THE DEFINITIVE CALIFORNIA BUCKET LIST

GUIDE BOOK

Over 110 Captivating Destinations and Discovery Nooks
to Transform Your Travel
Wishes into Everlasting Memories!
California Map & Journal

Sebastian Garcia

Credits

1. File Source: https://unsplash.com/it/foto/una-vista-del-golden-gate-bridge-dalla-spiaggia-dL2du5DXHeA
   License Details: https://unsplash.com/it/plus/licenza
   Author: Unsplash+ in collaboration with Joshua Earle
2. File Source: https://unsplash.com/it/foto/una-vista-di-una-spiaggia-da-una-scogliera-jtaDyKqr49k
   License Details: https://unsplash.com/it/licenza
   Author: Unsplash+ in collaboration with Getty Images
3. File Source: https://gisgeography.com/california-map/
   License Details: Free License for Educational and Commercial Uses
   Source: GISGeography.com
4. File Source: https://gisgeography.com/california-map/
   License Details: Free License for Educational and Commercial Uses
   Source: GISGeography.com
5. File Source: https://unsplash.com/it/foto/la-vista-del-faro-di-point-vicente-rancho-palos-verdes-california-usa-ajjMfOk4dRQ
   License Details: https://unsplash.com/it/plus/licenza
   Source: Unsplash+ in collaboration with Getty Images
6. File Source: https://unsplash.com/it/foto/photographie-a-plat-dun-appareil-photo-dun-livre-et-dun-sac-qyAka7W5uMY
   License Details: https://unsplash.com/it/licenza
   Author: Image by anniespratt
7. File Source: https://commons.wikimedia.org/wiki/File:Big_Sur_McWay_Falls_13.JPG
   License Details: https://creativecommons.org/licenses/by-sa/4.0/deed.en
   Author: Picture by Miguel Hermoso Cuesta
8. File Source: https://commons.wikimedia.org/wiki/File:Portal_of_the_Sun,_Pfeiffer_Beach,_Big_Sur,_California.jpg
   License Details: https://creativecommons.org/licenses/by/2.0/deed.en
   Author: Image by Jason Swearingen
9. File Source: https://commons.wikimedia.org/wiki/File:Death_Valley_Zabriskie_Point.jpg

License Details:
https://commons.wikimedia.org/wiki/Commons:GNU_Free_Doc
umentation_License,_version_1.2 -
https://creativecommons.org/licenses/by-sa/3.0/deed.en
Author: Picture by Wolfgangbeyer

10. File Source:
https://commons.wikimedia.org/wiki/File:Emerald_Bay_State_Park_
2.jpg
    License Details: https://creativecommons.org/licenses/by-
sa/4.0/deed.en
    Author: Public Domain

11. File Source:
https://commons.wikimedia.org/wiki/File:Hollywood_Highland_Wal
k_of_Fame.jpg
    License Details:
https://creativecommons.org/publicdomain/zero/1.0/deed.en
    Author: Picture of Luijtenphotos

12. File Source: https://commons.wikimedia.org/wiki/File:Castello-di-
Amorosa-front-2015.jpg
    License Details: https://creativecommons.org/licenses/by-
sa/4.0/deed.en
    Author: Picture of Photowikiuser816

13. File Source:
https://commons.wikimedia.org/wiki/File:We%27ve_got_to_stop_m
eeting_like_this,_Palm_Springs_Aerial_Tramway,_CA_2015_(2615
1516883).jpg
    License Details: https://creativecommons.org/licenses/by-
sa/2.0/deed.en
    Author: Source: Image by Don Graham from Redlands, CA,
USA - God bless it!

14. File Source:
https://commons.wikimedia.org/wiki/File:California_State_Capitol_(
2010-03-23).jpg
    License Details: https://creativecommons.org/licenses/by-
sa/4.0/deed.en
    Author: Picture of ©Steven Pavlov

15. File Source:
https://commons.wikimedia.org/wiki/File:Michigan_State_Capitol_0
1.jpg
    License Details: https://creativecommons.org/licenses/by-
sa/4.0/deed.en

Legal & Disclaimer © 2023

(1)

Table Of Contents

Discover the True Essence of California

(2)

California is a dream destination, right? With its incredible diversity of landscapes, cultures, and endless adventures, there's something for every type of traveler. But for first-timers, all that information out there can get overwhelming fast. Where do you even start to find the real California beyond the noise and tourist traps?

Lucky for you, this handy guide has got your back! As an insider Californian travel guru, I'll let you in on the quintessential Golden State experiences that truly capture the unique spirit of this magical place. Forget aimlessly googling - my recommendations come from extensive personal explorations and 100% honest reviews.

Inside you'll find my curated collection of must-visit destinations across California. I'll provide super clear maps so you always know where you're going and what's nearby. There's space to journal your memories, and pro tips to avoid common mistakes. Numerous happy travelers have said how useful these insider secrets are!

Whether you seek Big Sur's serenity, Napa Valley's indulgence, or big city excitement in L.A. and S.F., this guide's got you covered. Consider it your ticket to experiencing the real California in a mindful way - unfiltered, unrestrained, unforgettable. Of course destinations evolve, but the essence remains timeless.

The heart of California is waiting, my friend! Now is the perfect time to start planning your custom adventure. Use this guide to chart a course through California's soul and most jaw-dropping panoramas. Your journey begins right here...

The Map of California

(3)
Cities and Roads

(4)
Parks and Lakes

What Makes California So Special

(5)

Nicknamed the Golden State, California brews together nature, culture, and innovation to create one-of-a-kind experiences that entice travelers worldwide. Whether a seasoned pro or curious newcomer, California offers a treasure trove of diverse wonders waiting to be uncovered. Here's why California should top your destination wishlist:

1. **Captivating Landscapes:** California encapsulates the world's most breathtaking scenery, from Pacific Coast beaches to formidable Sierra peaks, surreal Death Valley deserts to Napa Valley vineyards. The iconic Highway 1 coastal drive is a scenic reverie encapsulating the state's natural grandeur.

2. **Cultural Fusion:** California celebrates global cultures, welcoming every tradition to find a home. Cities buzz with eclectic events, cuisines, art, and languages. Festivals, fairs, and concerts exude the inclusive spirit.

3. **Innovation Epicenter:** As the tech revolution's birthplace, California shapes the future and Silicon Valley symbolizes human ingenuity. Visiting offers a glimpse into an innovation-driven world.

4. **Historic Allure:** From ancient Redwood groves to Gold Rush towns, California beautifully blends past and present.

5. **Recreation Haven:** With endless activities like surfing, hiking and rock climbing, California is a paradise for outdoor enthusiasts. Vast national parks offer trails for all abilities.

6. **Culinary Adventure:** With thriving agro-industry, California tantalizes foodies with farm-to-table dining and world-class wineries.

7. **Engaging Education:** Diverse museums, galleries and tours provide enlightening, interactive learning.

8. **Iconic Symbols:** Lastly, landmarks like the Golden Gate Bridge, Hollywood Sign, and Disneyland are globally recognized Californian icons.

California is more than a destination - it's an experience, emotion and story waiting to unfold. Each visit promises diverse, dynamic memories as unique as the state itself. When wanderlust strikes, let California's trails satisfy your exploring urge. The magic awaits you to discover every shade and nuance. Your Golden State journey is sure to be a rewarding discovery.

How to Use this Book

(6)

This guidebook is thoughtfully designed to simplify planning your California adventure and make it more engaging. Let's explore how it's structured to put invaluable insights at your fingertips:

Map Guide: Inside the front cover you'll find a detailed California map to orient you geographically for the journey ahead. It's much more than labels - it lets you visualize where the state's gems lie at a glance. When a locale captures your interest, check the map to grasp its position within California's vast terrain.

City Sections: The guidebook is organized by city, laying out clear pathways to explore each area's unique offerings. Under every city header, I share my handpicked collection of must-see spots, each with distinct allure. This allows you to fully immerse in one area or bounce between cities - the choice is yours!

Location Entries: Now let's look inside each location entry:

- Why Visit - Distills the essence of what makes this place special.

- Best Time - Recommendations on ideal timing considering weather, events etc. to optimize your experience.
- Location - Concise geographic context to grasp its situation.
- Directions - Clear instructions to get there from the nearest landmark or town.
- Coordinates - Provided for tech-savvy travelers who prefer precision.
- Nearest Town - Details on a nearby base town for overnighting.
- Interesting Facts - Intriguing bits to enrich your visit with history and context.

The goal is to equip you with key details in an engaging way to make planning effortless and enjoyable. Each section artfully combines vital info, fascinating stories, and handy local tips to make your time in California truly unforgettable.

110 Places and Spots to Visit in California

ANAHEIM

Disneyland Resort

Why You Should Visit: Step into the magical realm of Disneyland Resort, where whimsy and wonder reign supreme. This canvas brings imagination to life through timeless tales and enchanted worlds. Visiting feels like walking through the pages of a living fairy tale, with laughter and dreams coming true around every corner. Meet your favorite characters, reunite with childhood nostalgia, and create new memories on rides like Space Mountain, It's a Small World, and Pirates of the Caribbean.

Best Time to Visit: September to December to avoid peak crowds.

Location: 1313 Disneyland Dr, AnaheimCalifornia.

Directions: From L.A. or Orange County, take I-5, exiting at Disneyland Drive, Ball Road or Harbor Blvd. Signs in Anaheim direct you to the resort. Use the Disneyland app for parking and traffic updates.

GPS Coordinates: 33.8121° N, 117.9190° W

Nearest Town: Anaheim

Interesting Facts: Disneyland Park opened July 17, 1955 as the only park Walt Disney personally designed and oversaw construction of.

Adventure City

Why You Should Visit: Though pint-sized, Adventure City packs a wallop of joy into its compact area, perfect for little thrill-seekers and families. With rides and attractions tailored to the whims of younger kids, it's a delightful world of fun designed just for them. Giggles and wide-eyed wonder abound as the kids experience the kid-friendly rides. Meander through and share the laughter and excitement of this charming, intimate park made for creating magical memories together.

Best Time to Visit: September to December to avoid crowds.

Location: 238 S Beach Blvd, Anaheim, California.

Directions: Adventure City is right off the 405 Freeway at Beach Blvd - just follow the signs toward the laughter and excitement!

GPS Coordinates: 33.8165° N, 117.9981° W

Nearest Town: Anaheim

Interesting Facts: Though small in scale compared to mega-parks, Adventure City has provided big joy and lasting memories since opening in 1994 - especially for younger kids and families seeking a charming, friendly experience.

Anaheim Packing District

Why You Should Visit: Take a leisurely stroll through the Anaheim Packing District, where history and modernity blend vibrantly. The former 1919 citrus packing house now hosts unique eateries and boutiques brimming with flavor and charm. Meander through this architectural gem, inhaling the aromas of fresh coffee, artisanal foods and Anaheim's eclectic local vibe. It's beyond a food hall - it's a lively gathering spot where tales of the past seamlessly mix with contemporary zeal.

Best Time to Visit: September through December.

Location: 440 S Anaheim Blvd, Anaheim, California.

Directions: Head to E. Anaheim Blvd and S. Claudina St to find this culinary and cultural beacon, with ample nearby parking.

GPS Coordinates: 33.8316° N, 117.9114° W

Nearest Town: Anaheim

Interesting Facts: The historic Packard Building here was a 1920s car showroom and now houses modern eateries, blending past and present in a beautifully restored citrus packing house.

Yorba Regional Park

Why You Should Visit: Yorba Regional Park is a 140-acre haven of greenery and serenity amid urban sprawl. Tranquil lakes, shaded picnic spots and winding paths offer refreshing natural recreation. Glide across the water, play volleyball, or spend a peaceful afternoon lakeside. The gentle rustling leaves, chirping birds and calm ambiance make Yorba a cherished spot to unwind.

Best Time to Visit: September through May.

Location: 7600 E La Palma Ave, Anaheim, California.

Directions: Take CA-91 E, exit at Weir Canyon Rd, right on E La Palma Ave to find this oasis.

GPS Coordinates: 33.8675° N, 117.7602° W

Nearest Town: Anaheim

Interesting Facts: Designed along the Santa Ana River with four interconnected lakes, Yorba Regional Park nods to the river's history and creates delightful aqueous pathways for visitors to enjoy the peaceful natural scenery.

Anaheim GardenWalk

Why You Should Visit: Anaheim GardenWalk blends outdoor shopping, dining, and entertainment into a vibrant hub to revel in Anaheim's culture. The open-air design is a canvas of colorful murals, boutiques, and diverse restaurants to suit every taste. As night falls, it transitions into a hub of nightlife with bars and exciting escape rooms. It's more than a shopping center - it's a leisure and amusement narrative awaiting you.

Best Time to Visit: March through June.

Location: 400 Disney Way, Anaheim, California.

Directions: Take I-5 S, exit 110A for Disney Way, right on Disney Way, right on S Anaheim Blvd, left on E Katella Ave. GardenWalk is on your right.

GPS Coordinates: 33.8031° N, 117.9153° W

Nearest Town: Anaheim

Interesting Facts: Anaheim GardenWalk is home to unique murals by renowned artists, turning a shopping spree into an immersive artistic journey.

BIG SUR

McWay Falls

(7)

Why You Should Visit: McWay Falls epitomizes Big Sur's untouched natural beauty, where a silvery cascade meets the calm Pacific. Water tumbles 80 feet off a cliff, forming a picturesque fall that settles on the sandy shore, crafting an almost surreal scene. The overlook trail frames this spectacular sight with endless ocean and rugged cliffs, captivating all.

Best Time to Visit: September to November.

Location: In Julia Pfeiffer Burns State Park along California's dramatic coast.

Directions: From Highway 1, exit for Julia Pfeiffer Burns State Park. Follow signs to the parking lot, then a short, marked trail to the overlook.

GPS Coordinates: 36.1589° N, 121.6720° W

Nearest Town: Carmel-by-the-Sea

Interesting Facts: McWay Falls previously cascaded directly into the ocean until a 1983 landslide created the sandy beach below, offering a new path for the waters to caress before meeting the waves.

Bixby Creek Bridge

Why You Should Visit: Bixby Creek Bridge is an iconic emblem of Big Sur's scenic and architectural splendor. More than just a bridge, it's a gateway to untamed beauty beyond. One of the world's tallest single-span concrete bridges elegantly arches over cliffs, offering a surreal drive with the Pacific raging below. The juxtaposition of craftsmanship and wild nature is astonishing, making it a photography haven.

Best Time to Visit: September to December.

Location: Along the Pacific Coast Highway (Highway 1), 15 miles south of Monterey and Carmel-by-the-Sea.

Directions: Bixby Creek Bridge is part of the scenic drive along Highway 1 from Monterey. Small parking areas near the bridge allow you to stop, admire the views, and photograph this iconic landmark.

GPS Coordinates: 36.3730° N, 121.9010° W

Nearest Town: Carmel-by-the-Sea

Interesting Facts: Completed in 1932, Bixby Creek Bridge quickly became one of the most photographed Pacific Coast bridges for its graceful design and dramatic vistas.

Pfeiffer Beach

(8)

Why You Should Visit: Pfeiffer Beach is no ordinary shoreline - it's a masterpiece where nature astonishes. Unique purple sand, courtesy of eroded manganese garnet deposits, sets a different tone under the sun. Towering rock formations, sculpted by relentless waves, stand guard along the shore, creating an otherworldly setting. The keyhole rock, with waves crashing through at sunset, offers magical photographic moments. This one-of-a-kind natural beauty is not to be missed.

Best Time to Visit: September to December.

Location: Off Highway 1 along the Big Sur coast.

Directions: From Highway 1, turn west onto easily missed Sycamore Canyon Road between Big Sur Station and Pfeiffer Big Sur State Park. Follow the winding road to the paid parking lot at the end.

GPS Coordinates: 36.2384° N, 121.8176° W

Nearest Town: Carmel-by-the-Sea

Interesting Facts: The purple sand is unique to Pfeiffer Beach, resulting from manganese garnet deposits in the hills eroding down to the shore over time.

Julia Pfeiffer Burns State Park

Why You Should Visit: Immerse yourself in wild Big Sur beauty at Julia Pfeiffer Burns State Park. This pristine sanctuary harbors majestic redwoods, dramatic waterfalls, and serene trails through diverse ecosystems. The crown jewel, McWay Falls, cascades gracefully onto a picturesque beach, epitomizing Big Sur's breathtaking beauty.

Best Time to Visit: April to October.

Location: Along the famed Highway 1, 37 miles south of Carmel.

Directions: From Carmel, drive south on Highway 1 for about 37 miles until you reach the well-marked park entrance.

GPS Coordinates: 36.169610° N, -121.678682° W

Nearest Town: Carmel

Interesting Facts: Named for pioneering Big Sur woman Julia Pfeiffer Burns, the park stretches from the coast into higher elevations, showcasing the region's diverse natural grandeur.

Point Sur State Historic Park

Why You Should Visit: Perched on a volcanic crag, Point Sur State Historic Park is a majestic meeting of wild Pacific waves and rugged cliffs. The iconic Point Sur Lighthouse, standing tall since 1889, guides sailors along the treacherous Big Sur coast. Take a guided tour back in time to learn about the lightstation's rich maritime history and spooky ghost tales. Breathtaking panoramic views from the rock offer a serene yet exhilarating escape.

Best Time to Visit: April to October.

Location: CA-1, Monterey, California.

Directions: From Carmel, take the scenic Pacific Coast Highway 1 south. The marked entrance and parking lot come up after about 30 minutes.

GPS Coordinates: 36.3069° N, 121.9006° W

Nearest Town: Carmel

Interesting Facts: The Point Sur Lighthouse is one of the only complete early 20th century lightstations open to the public in California. The rocky volcanic crag on which it stands contrasts starkly against the deep blue Pacific.

CARMEL-BY-THE-SEA

Carmel Beach

Why You Should Visit: Carmel Beach blends Carmel-by-the-Sea's artsy soul with the Pacific coast's splendor. This pristine white sandy beach is a peaceful retreat and picturesque sunset venue. Elegant cypress trees line the shore, while the charming town beckons exploring. Cozy by a bonfire, surf the waves, or soak up the sun - Carmel Beach embodies serenity and sublimity.

Best Time to Visit: March to May.

Location: At the foot of Ocean Avenue in Carmel-by-the-Sea.

Directions: From downtown Carmel, head west on Ocean Avenue to find the stunning Carmel Beach. Parking along Scenic Road.

GPS Coordinates: 36.5552° N, 121.9235° W

Nearest Town: Carmel-by-the-Sea

Interesting Facts: Known for welcoming dogs off-leash, Carmel Beach's uniquely soft, powdery white sand makes it a favorite of both locals and visitors.

Point Lobos State Natural Reserve

Why You Should Visit: Point Lobos State Natural Reserve is a haven for nature enthusiasts. Its hiking trails provide stunning views of the Pacific Ocean, while the underwater areas offer excellent scuba diving opportunities. It's a quiet place to appreciate California's rugged coastline.

Best Time to Visit: April through October.

Location: Central coast of California, Monterey County.

Directions: From Monterey, take CA-1 S for about 7.5 miles to reach the entrance to Point Lobos State Natural Reserve on your right.

GPS Coordinates: 36.5216° N, 121.9529° W

Nearest Town: Carmel-by-the-Sea

Interesting Facts: The Reserve hosts a historic whalers' cabin now turned museum. Its name, "Point Lobos," translates to "Point of the Sea Wolves," coined by early Spanish mariners due to the sea lions' barking sounds inhabiting the area.

Carmel Mission Basilica Museum

Why You Should Visit: Journey back in time to California's missionary era within the Carmel Mission Basilica Museum's serene walls. Beautifully preserved Spanish Baroque architecture and tranquil courtyards offer respite from the modern world. The museum brims with religious artifacts, art, and exhibits that interweave history, culture, and spirituality. Find enriching education and reverence for California's heritage.

Best Time to Visit: April to October.

Location: 3080 Rio Road, Carmel-By-The-Sea.

Directions: From Highway 1, exit onto Rio Road heading west to the mountains. After 1.5 miles, the museum is on your left.

GPS Coordinates: 36.5430° N, 121.9193° W

Nearest Town: Carmel-by-the-Sea

Interesting Facts: Founded in 1771 by Saint Junipero Serra, the Carmel Mission is one of California's oldest Spanish missions. Its stunning basilica captures the early settlers' spirit and architectural prowess as a designated National Historic Landmark.

Tor House and Hawk Tower

Why You Should Visit: Tor House and Hawk Tower romantically embody artistic expression and whimsical architecture on Carmel's rugged coast. These hand-built stone structures were the dream of famed poet Robinson Jeffers. Wandering through, feel the allure of the windswept shore, the whisper of Pacific winds, and echoes of Jeffers' timeless verses. A profound yet silent harmony of nature, art, and design.

Best Time to Visit: March to June.

Location: 26304 Ocean View Ave, Carmel-By-The-Sea.

Directions: From downtown Carmel, head west on 8th Ave, right on Monte Verde St, left on Ocean View Ave. Tor House and Hawk Tower will be on your right.

GPS Coordinates: 36.5485° N, 121.9305° W

Nearest Town: Carmel-by-the-Sea

Interesting Facts: Jeffers hand-built these structures from local granite boulders, reflecting his deep connection to the rugged California coast that he often wrote about in verse.

Carmel River State Beach

Why You Should Visit: Carmel River State Beach is a picturesque escape where the serene Carmel River meets the Pacific. Renowned for birdwatching and a vibrant marine sanctuary, this beach is a natural splendor sanctuary. Lapping waves against fine white sands make a soothing soundtrack for peaceful days under the sun, while nearby wetlands hum with rich biodiversity, beckoning nature lovers. The calm waters melodiously contrast the rugged backdrop of Monterey pines and cypress trees.

Best Time to Visit: April to October.

Location: 26478 Carmelo St, Carmel-By-The-Sea, CA 93923.

Directions: From downtown Carmel, head west on Ocean Ave, continue on Carmelo St, turn right staying on Carmelo to the beach.

GPS Coordinates: 36.5311° N, 121.9376° W

Nearest Town: Carmel-by-the-Sea

Interesting Facts: Part of the renowned Monterey Peninsula coastline and marine conservation efforts, Carmel River State Beach offers a window into the diverse Pacific marine life, including a vibrant kelp forest sheltering creatures.

DEATH VALLEY

Badwater Basin

Why You Should Visit: Badwater Basin, Death Valley's lowest point 282 feet below sea level, is a surreal salt flat that seems otherworldly. The vast expanse of crystalline salt stretches endlessly, starkly contrasting the surrounding rugged mountains and blue sky. It's a place where Earth shows its extremes, a captivating spectacle of natural wonder.

Best Time to Visit: November to March.

Location: Death Valley National Park, CA.

Directions: From Furnace Creek, take Badwater Road south about 17 miles until you reach the designated parking area. The basin is a short walk away.

GPS Coordinates: 36.2304° N, 116.7670° W

Nearest Town: Furnace Creek

Interesting Facts: Named for an undrinkable small spring pool where accumulated salts make the water unsuitable, Badwater Basin portrays Death Valley's stark yet beautiful resilience in extreme conditions.

Zabriskie Point

(9)

Why You Should Visit: Zabriskie Point unveils a panorama of rippling, eroded hill formations in pastel hues. As sunlight dances across these surreal shapes, a mesmerizing tableau emerges. Perched above vibrant badlands, the viewpoint offers a breathtaking perspective of Death Valley's rugged yet delicate landscapes. Feel the ancient whispers of the earth amid the desert's stillness.

Best Time to Visit: October to April.

Location: Death Valley National Park, CA.

Directions: From Furnace Creek, head southeast on CA-190 E for about 5 miles, turn left to Zabriskie Point road, continue to the parking lot. The viewpoint is a short walk away.

GPS Coordinates: 36.4201° N, 116.8103° W

Nearest Town: Furnace Creek

Interesting Facts: Named for a 20th century borax company executive, Zabriskie Point has been featured in films and music, adding to its cultural depiction of Death Valley's stark yet beautiful landscapes.

Dante's View

Why You Should Visit: Perched over 5,000 feet high, Dante's View unveils a panoramic spectacle of the Death Valley basin unfolding dramatically below your feet. Contrasting the highest Black Mountains peak with the valley's lowest point creates a surreal reminder of the Earth's geology. Take in the desert's vastness and serenity from this awe-inspiring vantage point.

Best Time to Visit: October to April.

Location: Death Valley National Park, CA.

Directions: From Furnace Creek, take CA-190 E about 12 miles, turn left onto Furnace Creek Wash Road, continue 13 miles on Dante's View Road following signs.

GPS Coordinates: 36.2211° N, 116.7266° W

Nearest Town: Furnace Creek

Interesting Facts: Named for Dante Alighieri's bleak, desolate portrayal of Hell, Dante's View offered panoramic shots of the planet Tatooine in 1977's Star Wars: A New Hope.

Mesquite Flat Sand Dunes

Why You Should Visit: Mesquite Flat Sand Dunes encapsulate Death Valley's quintessential desert vistas. Rolling dunes provide a surreal, picturesque setting perfect for photography and exploring. Strolling the sandy trails, the serene ambiance and ever-shifting shapes under the dancing sunlight create a captivating experience. A window into the valley's stark yet beautiful arid environment.

Best Time to Visit: November to April.

Location: Near Stovepipe Wells, Death Valley National Park.

Directions: From Furnace Creek, take CA-190 W about 22 miles to reach the parking area, following posted signs.

GPS Coordinates: 36.6061° N, 117.1150° W

Nearest Town: Stovepipe Wells

Interesting Facts: Among the most accessible dunes in the park, Mesquite Flat Sand Dunes offer a sense of solitude despite their popularity. The dunes house unique wildlife adapted to the harsh desert climate.

HUNTINGTON BEACH

Huntington State Beach

Why You Should Visit: Huntington State Beach epitomizes California's sun, sand, and surf culture. Extensive sandy shores, consistent waves, and a welcoming vibe create a paradise for beachgoers, surfers, and families. The iconic pier offers spectacular ocean views, surfing action, and glowing sunsets. Warm rays, salty breezes, and gentle waves provide serene escape from life's hustle. An essential for any California adventure.

Best Time to Visit: May to October.

Location: 21601 Pacific Coast Hwy, Huntington Beach, California.

Directions: From I-405, take the Beach Blvd exit south. Follow Beach Blvd to Pacific Coast Hwy where the park entrance awaits.

GPS Coordinates: 33.6500° N, 117.9876° W

Nearest Town: Huntington Beach

Interesting Facts: Nicknamed "Surf City USA," Huntington Beach hosts the annual US Open of Surfing, drawing surfers and spectators from around the globe.

Huntington Beach Pier

Why You Should Visit: Huntington Beach Pier is a symbol of the city's surfing culture and offers a classic Southern California experience. The pier provides a vantage point for watching surfers, enjoying sunsets, and taking in the vast Pacific horizon. At the end of the pier, you can find Ruby's Diner, where you can grab a bite while overlooking the ocean.

Best Time to Visit: Year-round, though summer months (June through August) offer warm weather and vibrant sunset views.

Location: Huntington Beach, Orange County, California.

Directions: From I-405, take exit 16 for Beach Blvd toward CA-39 S. Follow Beach Blvd for about 5.5 miles and turn left onto Pacific Coast Hwy. In about 0.3 miles, you'll reach Huntington Beach Pier area.

GPS Coordinates: 33.6569° N, 118.0029° W

Nearest Town: Huntington Beach

Interesting Facts: The pier has witnessed numerous reconstructions due to storm damage, with the current structure standing since 1992. It's one of the longest public piers on the West Coast, stretching 1,850 feet into the ocean. The pier also hosts the annual Vans US Open of Surfing, attracting the world's top surfers and a large audience eager to witness the competition amidst the historic backdrop of the Huntington Beach Pier.

Bolsa Chica Ecological Reserve

Why You Should Visit: Bolsa Chica Ecological Reserve is a breath of fresh air for nature and birding enthusiasts. Over 200 bird species inhabit this coastal wetland escape tucked amid the bustling city. Tranquil trails provide a serene backdrop for jogging, walking, or photographing. Whether you love nature, photography, or peaceful retreats, Bolsa Chica's sights and sounds offer resplendent respite.

Best Time to Visit: March to November.

Location: 8000 CA-1, Huntington Beach, California.

Directions: From I-405, exit onto Warner Ave westbound. At Pacific Coast Hwy, turn left - the reserve entrance is on the right.

GPS Coordinates: 33.7150° N, 118.0373° W

Nearest Town: Huntington Beach

Interesting Facts: As one of California's last remaining coastal wetlands, Bolsa Chica is a vital wildlife sanctuary and hub for environmental education and research.

Huntington Dog Beach

Why You Should Visit: Huntington Dog Beach welcomes furry friends with open paws. Golden sands, playful waves, and exhilarating off-leash freedom create a joyful haven for dogs to romp. While your loyal companion revels in the liberty, bask in the sun, join the playful camaraderie, or stroll the water's edge. This slice of paradise celebrates the unbreakable human-canine bond.

Best Time to Visit: May to October.

Location: 100 Goldenwest St, Huntington Beach, California.

Directions: Along Pacific Coast Hwy between Seapoint St and 21st St. From I-405, exit Goldenwest or Beach Blvd, drive toward the ocean, then left onto PCH.

GPS Coordinates: 33.6782° N, 118.0204° W

Nearest Town: Huntington Beach

Interesting Facts: Recognized as one of California's best dog beaches, Huntington Dog Beach fosters a community celebrating this precious off-leash space and the sheer joy it brings dogs and their humans.

International Surfing Museum

Why You Should Visit: The International Surfing Museum is a treasure chest capturing surfing's essence in California's cultural fabric. Step inside a tide of surfing history, where vintage boards tell tales of legendary waves and exhibits echo iconic surfers' adventures. More than a museum, it's a tribute to the surf culture defining Huntington Beach.

Best Time to Visit: March to October.

Location: 411 Olive Ave, Huntington Beach, California.

Directions: At 411 Olive Ave. From I-405, exit toward Beach Blvd, continue onto Center Ave, left onto Beach Blvd, right on Atlanta Ave, left on Olive Ave.

GPS Coordinates: 33.6601° N, 118.0017° W

Nearest Town: Huntington Beach

Interesting Facts: The museum nurtures Huntington Beach's vibrant surf culture through special events like the Surfing Sundays concert series and Surfing Walk of Fame induction ceremonies.

LAKE TAHOE

(10)

Emerald Bay State Park

Why You Should Visit: Embrace the allure of Lake Tahoe's crown jewel, Emerald Bay State Park, where serene emerald waters reflect the surrounding rugged peaks and azure sky in a picturesque tableau. Nature's artistry epitomized, with majestic Fannette Island standing guard over the tranquil bay. Each vista frames natural splendor, making this park a haven for scenic grandeur and tranquil escape.

Best Time to Visit: May to September.

Location: Lake Tahoe, California.

Directions: From South Lake Tahoe, head northwest on Emerald Bay Rd (CA-89) for about 9 miles, following signs to parking areas.

GPS Coordinates: 38.9517° N, 120.1067° W

Nearest Town: South Lake Tahoe

Interesting Facts: The park is home to Vikingsholm mansion, considered one of the finest examples of Scandinavian architecture in the U.S. This

38-room architectural marvel nestled at the head of Emerald Bay also testifies to the region's rich heritage.

Sand Harbor Beach

Why You Should Visit: Sand Harbor Beach is a paradise slice nestled along Lake Tahoe's eastern shore. Azure waters gently lap against the smooth, sandy shore, offering tranquil retreat for sun-seekers and water lovers. Rugged rock formations pepper the landscape, providing picturesque backdrops for relaxation or capturing Tahoe's natural beauty.

Best Time to Visit: June to August.

Location: Lake Tahoe, Nevada.

Directions: From Incline Village, take NV-28 S about 5 miles. Follow signs to Sand Harbor Beach State Park entrance.

GPS Coordinates: 39.1857° N, 119.9280° W

Nearest Town: Incline Village

Interesting Facts: Renowned for its clear waters, Sand Harbor provides excellent visibility for snorkeling and scuba diving. The water clarity also enhances the views, allowing visitors to peer into Lake Tahoe's depths from shore or paddleboards.

Heavenly Mountain Resort

Why You Should Visit: Heavenly Mountain Resort is a majestic escape that stands as a testament to Lake Tahoe's year-round allure. In winter, the resort transforms into a snowy wonderland, offering a multitude of trails for skiing and snowboarding. When the snow melts, a verdant landscape emerges, providing a playground for hiking, mountain biking, and zip-lining adventures. Its high-altitude location gifts visitors with breathtaking views of the crystalline Lake Tahoe and the surrounding mountain ranges, making it a picturesque retreat regardless of the season.

Best Time to Visit: For snow sports, from November to April; for summer activities, from June to September.

Location: 3860 Saddle Rd, South Lake Tahoe, California.

Directions: From South Lake Tahoe, head southwest on Lake Tahoe Blvd toward Emerald Bay Rd, then turn right onto Ski Run Blvd and follow the signs to Heavenly Mountain Resort.

GPS Coordinates: 38.9582° N, 119.9400° W

Nearest Town: South Lake Tahoe

Interesting Facts: Heavenly Mountain Resort boasts one of the largest ski areas in Lake Tahoe, with a total of 97 runs and 30 lifts. Its unique position straddling the California-Nevada state line allows visitors to ski or ride down the slopes in two states in a single day.

Tahoe Rim Trail

Why You Should Visit: The 165-mile Tahoe Rim Trail loops around pristine Lake Tahoe, inviting adventure through diverse ecosystems and panoramic vistas. Traversing forests, alpine meadows, and rugged peaks unveils new perspectives of the Sierra Nevada and Carson ranges. Shared by hikers, bikers, and equestrians, it ensures a vibrant outdoor experience.

Best Time to Visit: June to October.

Location: Lake Tahoe Basin, California and Nevada.

Directions: Many access points around the lake. A popular trailhead is Tahoe Meadows, off NV-431 W/Mt Rose Hwy from Reno.

GPS Coordinates: 39.3122° N, 119.8972° W (Tahoe Meadows Trailhead)

Nearest Town: Incline Village, Nevada.

Interesting Facts: Intersecting with the iconic Pacific Crest Trail, the Tahoe Rim Trail offers avid hikers a chance to extend adventures through the scenic American West.

Vikingsholm

Why You Should Visit: Nestled at Emerald Bay's head, Vikingsholm is a Scandinavian architectural marvel in California's heart. This historic mansion offers early 20th-century elegance and legacy of Emerald Bay's once prestigious summer home. The serene setting and meticulous craftsmanship transport you to a distant Nordic landscape, making it a unique cultural and historical gem amid Lake Tahoe's natural beauty.

Best Time to Visit: May to September.

Location: Emerald Bay State Park, Lake Tahoe, California.

Directions: From South Lake Tahoe, take Highway 89 north about 8.5 miles. Parking lot and trailhead are at the far end.

GPS Coordinates: 38.9514° N, 120.1064° W

Nearest Town: South Lake Tahoe

Interesting Facts: Built in 1929 by Lora Josephine Knight, Vikingsholm blends Norse and Swedish architecture as a prime U.S. example of Scandinavian style.

LONG BEACH

Aquarium of the Pacific

Why You Should Visit: The Aquarium of the Pacific brings the mysteries of the deep to life before your eyes. This aquatic haven homes over 11,000 animals representing 500+ species, offering a dive into the undersea world without getting wet.

Best Time to Visit: September to May.

Location: 100 Aquarium Way, Long Beach, California.

Directions: Located at 100 Aquarium Way, Long Beach, CA 90802, just a short drive from downtown.

GPS Coordinates: 33.7620° N, 118.1967° W

Nearest Town: Long Beach

Interesting Facts: The Aquarium is known for its Shark Lagoon and Lorikeet Forest, delivering up-close encounters that create an immersive, educational experience for visitors of all ages.

Queen Mary

Why You Should Visit: The Queen Mary is a floating monument to a bygone era, a majestic British ocean liner now iconic on Long Beach's waterfront. With its storied past and ghostly legends, it blends history and mystery, offering a unique window into maritime heritage and wartime adventures.

Best Time to Visit: May to August.

Location: Docked permanently in Long Beach, California.

Directions: Located at 1126 Queens Highway, Long Beach, CA 90802, easily accessible from the city.

GPS Coordinates: 33.7526° N, 118.1893° W

Nearest Town: Long Beach

Interesting Facts: During WWII, the Queen Mary served as a troopship, earning the nickname "The Grey Ghost" for her stealthy grey exterior.

Long Beach Waterfront

Why You Should Visit: The Long Beach Waterfront is a picturesque Pacific stretch blending serene ocean views and a bustling harbor. Where the city meets the sea, with parks, paths, and vibrant atmosphere. It's perfect for leisurely strolls, scenic runs, or relaxing waterside - all with views of the iconic Queen Mary and lively port.

Best Time to Visit: April to October.

Location: Long Beach, California.

Directions: Accessible from many Long Beach points. A popular start is near the Aquarium of the Pacific to wander the scenic shores and Rainbow Harbor.

GPS Coordinates: 33.7607° N, 118.1957° W

Nearest Town: Long Beach

Interesting Facts: As home to many annual events and festivals, the Long Beach Waterfront creates a hub of cultural and maritime celebration in the city.

Naples Island

Why You Should Visit: Naples Island offers charming Italian-inspired enclave amid Long Beach's urban sprawl. With picturesque canals, gondola rides, and quaint paths, it's like a European village escape. The unique architectural styles and serene waterways make it a delightful, romantic destination.

Best Time to Visit: April to June, September to November.

Location: Long Beach, California.

Directions: Accessible from 2nd Street in Long Beach, turning onto Naples Plaza and crossing the Neapolitan Lane bridge.

GPS Coordinates: 33.7530° N, 118.1236° W

Nearest Town: Long Beach

Interesting Facts: Built on three Alamitos Bay islands in the early 1900s with the vision of creating an American Venice, Naples Island became a picturesque neighborhood of canals and beautiful homes exuding Italian charm.

El Dorado Nature Center

Why You Should Visit: El Dorado Nature Center is an urban oasis of natural beauty in Long Beach. Tranquil lakes, lush woodland trails, and diverse local flora and fauna offer a breath of fresh air. Whether you seek peaceful strolls, birdwatching, or learning about ecosystems, it's a respite from the city bustle.

Best Time to Visit: March to May, October to November.

Location: 7550 E Spring St, Long Beach, California.

Directions: Located at 7550 E Spring St, accessible via I-605 exiting Spring St eastbound.

GPS Coordinates: 33.8097° N, 118.0868° W

Nearest Town: Long Beach

Interesting Facts: Spanning 105 acres with nearly 2 miles of trails, El Dorado Nature Center provides a space for peaceful walks and environmental education. Its quaint museum sheds light on local ecology and conservation.

LOS ANGELES

Hollywood Walk of Fame

(11)

Why You Should Visit: The Hollywood Walk of Fame embodies entertainment's rich heritage, offering tactile connection to legendary stars. Along 15 blocks of Hollywood Boulevard, over 2,600 brass stars embedded in pink terrazzo honor luminaries of film, TV, radio, theater, and music. It's more than a sidewalk - it's tribute to pop culture icons.

Best Time to Visit: November to April.

Location: Hollywood Boulevard, Los Angeles.

Directions: Accessible by Metro Red Line at Hollywood/Vine or Hollywood/Highland, or by car with nearby parking.

GPS Coordinates: 34.0928° N, 118.3287° W

Nearest Town: Los Angeles

Interesting Facts: Initiated in 1958 with new stars added regularly, the Walk of Fame has become an enduring tribute to ongoing entertainment contributions. Each star's unveiling is a celebrated event often attended by honorees and fans.

Griffith Observatory

Why You Should Visit: Perched atop Mount Hollywood, Griffith Observatory grants stellar views of L.A. blended with rich astronomy experiences. This gateway to the cosmos offers fascinating exhibits, planetarium shows, and peering through the iconic Zeiss telescope. Gazing at stars or cityscapes, it's a celestial experience.

Best Time to Visit: September to May.

Location: 2800 E Observatory Rd, Los Angeles.

Directions: Drive up Vermont Ave or Fern Dell Dr, or take the DASH Observatory Bus.

GPS Coordinates: 34.1184° N, 118.3004° W

Nearest Town: Los Angeles

Interesting Facts: A 1935 gift to L.A. from Griffith J. Griffith to make astronomy public, Griffith Observatory houses a Tesla coil and its front lawn is a popular Hollywood Sign viewing spot.

Santa Monica Pier

Why You Should Visit: Santa Monica Pier is a vibrant coastal emblem inviting amusement - from the historic carousel to Pacific Park's Ferris wheel and aquarium. Beyond fun, it's where sun-kissed Pacific horizons meet Route 66's end, blending natural beauty with iconic Americana.

Best Time to Visit: May to October.

Location: 200 Santa Monica Pier, Santa Monica.

Directions: Accessible via Colorado Ave, with nearby parking. Also reachable by Big Blue Bus or Metro Expo Line.

GPS Coordinates: 34.0094° N, 118.4973° W

Nearest Town: Santa Monica

Interesting Facts: Pacific Park houses the world's only solar-powered Ferris wheel, bringing eco-friendly spin to the pier's traditional seaside amusement.

Venice Beach

Why You Should Visit: Venice Beach encapsulates SoCal culture with its freewheeling spirit. The iconic boardwalk bustles with street performers, vendors, and muscle beach gym, while serene sands and surf offer tranquil escape. More than just a beach, it's a theater of life's eccentricities under the sun.

Best Time to Visit: May to October.

Location: Venice, Los Angeles.

Directions: Between Santa Monica and Marina del Rey, accessible by car or public transport like Metro Bus 33. If driving, take I-10 west to Pacific Coast Highway.

GPS Coordinates: 33.9850° N, 118.4695° W

Nearest Town: Venice

Interesting Facts: Known for its Bohemian vibe, Venice Beach's vibrant community of performers, vendors, and muscle beach gymnasts showcase talents along the iconic boardwalk.

Getty Center

Why You Should Visit: The Getty Center is a remarkable hilltop monument of culture, art and architecture with panoramic L.A. views. Housing an extensive European painting, sculpture and decorative arts collection, it's a voyage through history's corridors. Meticulous gardens and contemporary designs enrich the experience, rendering a serene escape from city buzz.

Best Time to Visit: March to June.

Location: 1200 Getty Center Dr, Los Angeles, California.

Directions: At 1200 Getty Center Drive, near the 405 and 10 freeway intersection. Reachable by car, bus or taxi.

GPS Coordinates: 34.0780° N, 118.4740° W

Nearest Town: Los Angeles

Interesting Facts: Designed by Richard Meier, the Getty Center's architecture complements a central garden conceived by Robert Irwin as an evolving seasonal art piece.

MALIBU

Zuma Beach

Why You Should Visit: Known for long, wide sandy shores and excellent surf, Zuma Beach is a haven for beachgoers and surf enthusiasts. Sparkling waters, beautiful sunsets, and lively atmosphere encapsulate the quintessential Malibu experience. Catch waves, play beach volleyball, or just relax by the ocean - Zuma welcomes you.

Best Time to Visit: May to October.

Location: Malibu, California.

Directions: Off Pacific Coast Hwy at 30000 PCH, about 2 miles north of Kanan Dume Rd. Follow PCH to Bonsall Dr for the entrance.

GPS Coordinates: 34.0259° N, 118.7798° W

Nearest Town: Malibu

Interesting Facts: With its iconic backdrop of Southern California beach culture, Zuma Beach has been featured in numerous movies and TV shows over the years.

Malibu Creek State Park

Why You Should Visit: Nestled in the Santa Monica Mountains, Malibu Creek State Park is a nature lover's paradise. Sprawling wilderness, serene creeks, and hiking trails testify to the natural beauty thriving amid urban areas. Escape the city, indulge in birdwatching and hiking, or bask in nature's calmness.

Best Time to Visit: March to May.

Location: 1925 Las Virgenes Road, Calabasas, California.

Directions: Located at 1925 Las Virgenes Rd in Calabasas. From 101 take Las Virgenes Rd south, or from PCH go north.

GPS Coordinates: 34.0978° N, 118.7319° W

Nearest Town: Malibu

Interesting Facts: Once part of the 20th Century Fox Ranch used for filming classics like *Planet of the Apes*, the park's cinematic history adds to its rich natural allure.

Point Dume State Beach

Why You Should Visit: Point Dume State Beach strikes a balance of rugged cliffs standing guard over serene Pacific shores. It's the perfect spot for peaceful retreat - watch the sunset, spot sea lions and dolphins, explore tide pools. Point Dume offers engaging yet tranquil beach experiences.

Best Time to Visit: May to October.

Location: Malibu, California.

Directions: From Santa Monica, take PCH north to Westward Beach Road. Go past fee station to the road's end.

GPS Coordinates: 34.0012° N, 118.8065° W

Nearest Town: Malibu

Interesting Facts: Point Dume's cliffs and rock formations were featured in the 1968 film *Planet of the Apes*, adding cinematic history to the natural beauty.

Adamson House and Malibu Lagoon Museum

Why You Should Visit: The Adamson House and Malibu Lagoon Museum beautifully exemplify early 20th-century Spanish Colonial Revival architecture where Malibu Creek meets the Pacific. This historic home and museum offer a window into California's past through unique Malibu Potteries tilework and panoramic lagoon and ocean views. It's where history, art, and nature converge for an enriching experience.

Best Time to Visit: March to June.

Location: 23200 Pacific Coast Hwy, Malibu, California.

Directions: Located at 23200 Pacific Coast Highway, accessible from PCH coming from Santa Monica or Santa Barbara.

GPS Coordinates: 34.0259° N, 118.7738° W

Nearest Town: Malibu

Interesting Facts: Nicknamed the "Taj Mahal of Tile" for its extensive, exquisite decorative tilework considered among the finest in the world.

El Matador Beach

Why You Should Visit: El Matador Beach, a somewhat hidden Malibu gem, is adorned with sea caves and uniquely shaped rocks jutting from soft sands. It's a picturesque, ethereal spot perfect for photography, romantic sunset strolls, or escaping crowds. Dramatic cliffs and crashing waves create a captivating, almost ethereal atmosphere.

Best Time to Visit: May to October.

Location: 32350 Pacific Coast Hwy, Malibu, California.

Directions: Off PCH, a small brown sign marks the steep path down to the beach - wear sturdy shoes!

GPS Coordinates: 34.0250° N, 118.7795° W

Nearest Town: Malibu

Interesting Facts: Despite its hidden location, El Matador's dramatic landscape often draws photographers and filmmakers, as it's one of three beaches within Robert H. Meyer Memorial State Beach.

MONO LAKE

Mono Lake Tufa State Natural Reserve

Why You Should Visit: The Mono Lake Tufa State Natural Reserve is a geological wonderland. Tufa towers - spires and knobs formed by freshwater springs and alkaline lake water - create an otherworldly landscape. This vital habitat also hosts migratory birds feasting on abundant alkali flies. The lake's tranquil dawn and dusk serenity coupled with the eerie tufas offer a surreal experience.

Best Time to Visit: July to September.

Location: US-395, Lee Vining, California.

Directions: East on Highway 395, take the Mono Basin Scenic Area Visitor Center exit and follow signs.

GPS Coordinates: 38.0094° N, 119.0123° W

Nearest Town: Lee Vining

Interesting Facts: One of North America's oldest lakes with a unique ecosystem, the towering tufa formations reaching over 30 feet tall have been developing for centuries.

Mono Basin Scenic Area Visitor Center

Why You Should Visit: The Mono Basin Scenic Area Visitor Center is an excellent starting point to explore Mono Lake. Immersive exhibits explain the natural and human history before venturing into the starkly beautiful landscape. It's a gateway to understanding the area's geological, ecological, and historical significance. Panoramic views make it a perfect photography spot.

Best Time to Visit: June to September.

Location: 1 Visitor Center Dr, Lee Vining.

Directions: Off Highway 395 north of Lee Vining, follow signs to the visitor center exit.

GPS Coordinates: 37.9530° N, 119.1190° W

Nearest Town: Lee Vining

Interesting Facts: Operated by the US Forest Service, the center's spectacular vantage point high above Mono Lake offers expansive basin views. It also features a bookstore for delving deeper into the fascinating local lore.

Black Point Fissures

Why You Should Visit: Black Point Fissures offer a geologically distinctive hiking experience. Deep fissures - cracks in volcanic rock - provide adventurous exploration amidst surreal landscapes. Hiking here reveals panoramic Mono Lake basin views, rewarding those seeking unique natural phenomena.

Best Time to Visit: May to October.

Location: Northern shore of Mono Lake.

Directions: From Highway 395, take the Cemetery Road exit east, follow signs to Black Point parking area and trailhead.

GPS Coordinates: 38.0075° N, 119.0329° W

Nearest Town: Lee Vining

Interesting Facts: Formed by volcanic activity and molten rock interacting with Mono Lake's cold water, these deep earth cracks showcase dramatic geological forces at work.

Mono Lake Committee Information Center & Bookstore

Why You Should Visit: The Mono Lake Committee Information Center & Bookstore is a hub of knowledge for understanding Mono Lake's ecology, history and geology. It provides maps, guides and insights, making it a great starting point to explore the area. The bookstore offers literature and souvenirs to take Mono Lake's mystique home.

Best Time to Visit: April to November.

Location: 51359 US-395, Lee Vining, California.

Directions: On Highway 395 at Mono Lake's northwest corner. Take the Mono Lake exit and follow signs.

GPS Coordinates: 37.9573° N, 119.1197° W

Nearest Town: Lee Vining

Interesting Facts: The Mono Lake Committee works to protect, restore and educate about the Mono Lake ecosystem. Through the Information Center & Bookstore, they foster deeper understanding and appreciation of this unique saline lake.

Old Marina

Why You Should Visit: Old Marina is a quaint, less-frequented spot along Mono Lake's shores offering serene nature escape. Enjoy the calm waters, observe tufas up close, and soak in the picturesque views. It's perfect for photography and peaceful retreat.

Best Time to Visit: May to October.

Location: Northwestern shores of Mono Lake.

Directions: From Highway 395, take the Mono Lake exit and follow signs to Old Marina.

GPS Coordinates: 37.9625° N, 119.1289° W

Nearest Town: Lee Vining

Interesting Facts: Lesser-known than other Mono Lake areas, Old Marina allows you to experience the lake's tranquility and beauty without crowds. It's also a top birdwatching spot, especially during migration seasons when diverse species stop by.

NAPA VALLEY

Castello di Amorosa

(12)

Why You Should Visit: Castello di Amorosa is more than a winery - it's a remarkable medieval Italian castle recreated in picturesque Napa Valley. Authentic architecture with drawbridge, moat and dungeon, paired with exquisite wines, makes you feel transported back in time while indulging in California's finest.

Best Time to Visit: September to November.

Location: 4045 St Helena Hwy, Calistoga, Napa Valley, California.

Directions: Located at 4045 St Helena Hwy in Calistoga. Well-signed along St. Helena Hwy in either direction.

GPS Coordinates: 38.5584° N, 122.5427° W

Nearest Town: Calistoga

Interesting Facts: Meticulously crafted over 14 years to replicate a Tuscan castle, Castello di Amorosa boasts 107 rooms, a moat, drawbridge and torture chamber, blending authentic medieval charm with modern winemaking.

Sterling Vineyards

Why You Should Visit: Sterling Vineyards offers a one-of-a-kind wine tasting experience. Nestled in Napa Valley's verdant hills, an aerial tram whisks you up to the winery, revealing breathtaking views of the vineyards below. At the top, savor exquisite wines overlooking the picturesque landscape the region is known for.

Best Time to Visit: September to November.

Location: Calistoga, Napa Valley, California.

Directions: Located at 1111 Dunaweal Lane off CA-29, follow signs to the winery.

GPS Coordinates: 38.5796° N, 122.5776° W

Nearest Town: Calistoga

Interesting Facts: Inspired by Mykonos, Greece, Sterling's architecture reflects that Mediterranean charm. The aerial tram is a unique, exciting way to start your wine tasting adventure.

Domaine Carneros

Why You Should Visit: Domaine Carneros is renowned for exquisite sparkling wines and an elegant chateau nestled in Napa's rolling hills. Sip fine wine on the terrace while enjoying panoramic vineyard views under the California sun. A taste of French sophistication in the heart of Napa Valley.

Best Time to Visit: September to November.

Location: 1240 Duhig Rd, Napa, California.

Directions: Located at 1240 Duhig Rd, accessible from downtown Napa via CA-12/CA-121.

GPS Coordinates: 38.2554° N, 122.3547° W

Nearest Town: Napa

Interesting Facts: With its French chateau and founding by the Taittinger Champagne family, Domaine Carneros offers a slice of France in Napa.

Its focus on sparkling wines provides a quintessential Napa Valley experience.

Oxbow Public Market

Why You Should Visit: Oxbow Public Market is Napa Valley's local hub for fresh, artisanal, and gourmet food and drink. With a vibrant, bustling atmosphere, it's a haven for foodies to explore diverse culinary offerings. From produce stands to unique eateries and boutique wine shops, there's something for everyone to savor under one roof.

Best Time to Visit: September to November.

Location: 610 1st St, Napa, California.

Directions: Located at 610 1st St in downtown Napa, accessible via Main St and 1st St.

GPS Coordinates: 38.2992° N, 122.2855° W

Nearest Town: Napa

Interesting Facts: Encompassing 40,000 square feet with varied vendors, Oxbow Public Market showcases Napa Valley's agricultural bounty and gourmet foods. It's where locals and visitors gather to shop, socialize, and enjoy the community vibe.

Napa Valley Wine Train

Why You Should Visit: Riding the Napa Valley Wine Train feels like stepping back to a time of elegance, gliding past vineyards in restored vintage rail cars while savoring gourmet meals. This unforgettable journey tantalizes your taste buds as you experience stunning wine country in a truly unique way. It's not just a train ride - it's a sophisticated trip through Napa's best.

Best Time to Visit: September to November.

Location: 1275 McKinstry St, Napa, California.

Directions: Departs from 1275 McKinstry St in downtown Napa.

GPS Coordinates: 38.3075° N, 122.2844° W

Nearest Town: Napa

Interesting Facts: The Wine Train offers various excursions including murder mysteries, lunch/dinner tours, and vintner tours. The early 20th century rail cars add old-world charm to experiencing Napa Valley's treasures.

OAKLAND

Lake Merritt

Why You Should Visit: Lake Merritt sparkles as a peaceful urban oasis in Oakland's heart. The 3.4-mile heart-shaped shoreline offers jogging, picnicking and bird-watching, being a migratory bird sanctuary. Lush gardens, a whimsical children's theme park, and tranquil waters make Lake Merritt a delightful retreat.

Best Time to Visit: April to October.

Location: Oakland, California.

Directions: Located near downtown Oakland, bounded by Grand Ave and Lakeshore Ave among others. Multiple entry points surround the lake.

GPS Coordinates: 37.8044° N, 122.2712° W

Nearest Town: Oakland

Interesting Facts: Named the United States' first official wildlife refuge in 1870, Lake Merritt holds historical significance in urban wildlife conservation.

Oakland Museum of California

Why You Should Visit: The Oakland Museum of California fascinates as an amalgam of art, history and science exploring California's cultural and environmental heritage through engaging exhibits. With over 1.9 million objects spanning collections, it richly educates on the extraordinary California story.

Best Time to Visit: Year-round

Location: 1000 Oak St, Oakland, CA 94607

Directions: Located in downtown Oakland, accessible by car or public transit like the nearby Lake Merritt BART station.

GPS Coordinates: 37.7986° N, 122.2644° W

Nearest Town: Oakland

Interesting Facts: The museum hosts a popular weekly Friday Nights at OMCA event with half-price admission, live music, food trucks and family activities, creating a lively community gathering.

Oakland Zoo

Why You Should Visit: Oakland Zoo is a delightful wildlife haven and family spot. Home to over 750 native and exotic animals, it blends education with fun. Dedicated to conservation, it provides natural habitats - making it a beautiful place to explore the animal kingdom.

Best Time to Visit: March to May.

Location: 9777 Golf Links Rd, Oakland, CA 94605

Directions: Located in Oakland, accessible by car or bus from Coliseum BART station.

GPS Coordinates: 37.7516° N, 122.1477° W

Nearest Town: Oakland

Interesting Facts: A unique aerial gondola ride takes you above animal enclosures, offering a bird's-eye view of the entire zoo and surrounding wildlands from a new perspective.

Jack London Square

Why You Should Visit: Jack London Square is a vibrant Oakland waterfront destination steeped in history, entertainment, and scenic views. Named for the famous author who spent time here, it's a lively hub for dining, shopping, and activities. With its picturesque Oakland estuary setting, it's delightful for exploring, al fresco dining, or soaking up the sunny California ambiance.

Best Time to Visit: April to October.

Location: Broadway, Oakland, CA 94607

Directions: Easily accessible by car, BART, ferry, or bike, with dedicated parking and a short walk from Downtown Oakland.

GPS Coordinates: 37.7937° N, 122.2781° W

Nearest Town: Oakland

Interesting Facts: Jack London, famous for "The Call of the Wild" and "White Fang", spent his youth in this historic area. A replica of his Yukon cabin is on display, offering a glimpse into the adventurous author's life.

Redwood Regional Park

Why You Should Visit: Tucked just beyond Oakland, Redwood Regional Park is a hidden natural oasis of ancient redwoods, providing tranquil escape from the urban hustle. Meandering trails through towering redwoods, meadows, and streams offer rejuvenating hikes, bikes, or picnics under the canopy.

Best Time to Visit: April to October.

Location: 7867 Redwood Rd, Oakland, CA 94619

Directions: From Highway 13 take the Redwood Rd exit east uphill. The main entrance is on the right at the top.

GPS Coordinates: 37.8092° N, 122.1668° W

Nearest Town: Oakland

Interesting Facts: This park was heavily logged in the 1800s, but today houses a resilient second growth of redwoods that sprouted from the stumps, testifying to nature's power.

PALM SPRINGS

Palm Springs Aerial Tramway

(13)

Why You Should Visit: The Palm Springs Aerial Tramway offers a thrilling ride up over rugged Chino Canyon cliffs to pristine Mt. San Jacinto wilderness. At the top, a cooler climate awaits for hiking, picnicking or soaking up panoramic Coachella Valley views. This sky-high adventure is a must-experience.

Best Time to Visit: November to April.

Location: 1 Tram Way, Palm Springs, CA 92262

Directions: A short drive north of downtown Palm Springs on N Palm Canyon Dr, left on Tramway Rd leads to the valley station.

GPS Coordinates: 33.8374° N, 116.6140° W

Nearest Town: Palm Springs

Interesting Facts: Holding the record as the world's largest rotating tram car, the Palm Springs Tramway's slow rotation offers a 360-degree view for all passengers during the ascent.

Indian Canyons

Why You Should Visit: The Indian Canyons interweave natural splendors and cultural history as ancestral home of the Agua Caliente Cahuilla. Trails wander through serene palm oases, along streams, and under giant palms. Whispering breezes and trickling streams create a divine, tranquil retreat from bustle.

Best Time to Visit: November to April.

Location: 38520 S Palm Canyon Dr, Palm Springs, CA

Directions: From central Palm Springs, head south on S Palm Canyon Dr - entrance is on the left.

GPS Coordinates: 33.7701° N, 116.5453° W

Nearest Town: Palm Springs

Interesting Facts: Home to the Cahuilla for thousands of years, these trails were once walked by ancient tribes who used bedrock mortars along the way to grind grains.

Palm Springs Air Museum

Why You Should Visit: The Palm Springs Air Museum is a living tribute to past air warriors, housing one of the world's largest collections of flyable WWII aircraft. History takes flight where veterans share firsthand experiences, bringing tales of valor to life. It's an ode to aviation evolution and the brave pilots who manned these machines.

Best Time to Visit: November to April.

Location: 745 N Gene Autry Trail, Palm Springs, CA

Directions: From downtown Palm Springs, head north on N Palm Canyon Dr, left on E Vista Chino, right on N Gene Autry Trail.

GPS Coordinates: 33.8323° N, 116.5072° W

Nearest Town: Palm Springs

Interesting Facts: Along with the awe-inspiring aircraft, the museum hosts airshows and flight exhibitions where the vintage planes often take to the skies, thrilling aviation enthusiasts.

Moorten Botanical Garden

Why You Should Visit: Moorten Botanical Garden is a serene Palm Springs oasis showcasing diverse desert plants. Amid the bustling city, this tranquil garden transports you to a calm, picturesque desert landscape. With over 3,000 desert plant examples, it's a living museum of botanical wonders. The rare species "Cactarium" is a highlight, making it a plant lover's paradise and peaceful retreat.

Best Time to Visit: November to March.

Location: 1701 S Palm Canyon Dr, Palm Springs, CA

Directions: From downtown Palm Springs, head south on S Palm Canyon Dr - the garden is on the right.

GPS Coordinates: 33.8007° N, 116.5488° W

Nearest Town: Palm Springs

Interesting Facts: Established in 1938, Moorten Botanical Garden has been a cherished Hollywood celebrity destination for experiencing desert flora beauty.

Palm Springs Art Museum

Why You Should Visit: Palm Springs Art Museum offers insightful dives into contemporary art, architecture and design through engaging exhibits and impressive collections. The artwork spans cultures and eras, reflecting rich artistic heritage. The architecture seamlessly blends with natural surroundings, itself a work of art.

Best Time to Visit: Year-round

Location: 101 Museum Drive, Palm Springs, CA

Directions: Located downtown, accessible by car or transit. Nearby parking available.

GPS Coordinates: 33.8207° N, 116.5470° W

Nearest Town: Palm Springs

Interesting Facts: With a theater and free admission Thursdays, the museum makes art accessible. Its design-focused approach creates a unique Palm Springs spot to explore art, architecture and design.

PASADENA

The Huntington Library, Art Museum, and Botanical Gardens

Why You Should Visit: The Huntington is a trinity of cultural and natural enrichment. Wander exquisite gardens, explore vast art collections, and dive into historical texts. The botanical gardens provide serene escape with themed areas like the Japanese, Desert, and Chinese Gardens, each offering different aesthetic experiences.

Best Time to Visit: October to April.

Location: 1151 Oxford Road, San Marino, CA 91108

Directions: A short drive from Pasadena with onsite parking. Public transit available.

GPS Coordinates: 34.1290° N, 118.1140° W

Nearest Town: Pasadena

Interesting Facts: The Huntington hosts a remarkable rare book and manuscript collection including a Gutenberg Bible and early Canterbury Tales, making it a vibrant center of research and education.

Norton Simon Museum

Why You Should Visit: The Norton Simon Museum is an art treasure trove, housing an impressive collection spanning centuries and continents. It showcases European art from the Renaissance to modern day, plus a distinct Asian art collection from India, China and Japan. The tranquil sculpture garden offers peaceful retreat.

Best Time to Visit: Year-round.

Location: 411 W Colorado Blvd, Pasadena, CA 91105

Directions: Near the Pasadena Freeway, with free parking. Also accessible by Metro L Line to Memorial Park Station.

GPS Coordinates: 34.1457° N, 118.1601° W

Nearest Town: Pasadena

Interesting Facts: The museum is renowned for its remarkable Impressionist and Post-Impressionist collection, including works by Van Gogh, Degas, and Rembrandt, making it a must-see for art enthusiasts.

Rose Bowl Stadium

Why You Should Visit: The iconic Rose Bowl Stadium symbolizes Pasadena's rich sports history. Known for hosting the annual Rose Bowl Game and memorable concerts, soccer matches, and events, it fuses excitement and tradition. Its classic design and surrounding Brookside Park greenery create a one-of-a-kind venue.

Best Time to Visit: September to December during football season, or for special events.

Location: 1001 Rose Bowl Dr, Pasadena, CA 91103

Directions: Accessible via the 210 Freeway, exiting at Seco/Mountain and following signs. Also reachable by bus.

GPS Coordinates: 34.1610° N, 118.1676° W

Nearest Town: Pasadena

Interesting Facts: A National Historic Landmark with over 88,000 seats, the Rose Bowl has hosted 5 Super Bowls and the 1984 Olympic soccer matches.

Kidspace Children's Museum

Why You Should Visit: For family fun, Kidspace Children's Museum is a must-visit interactive wonderland. With over 40 hands-on exhibits, it's designed to ignite creativity and foster a lifelong love of learning through play. From Physics Forest to Arroyo Adventure, every corner provides engaging, educational experiences.

Best Time to Visit: Year-round.

Location: 480 N Arroyo Blvd, Pasadena, CA 91103

Directions: Accessible via the 210 Freeway, exiting at Del Mar Blvd or California Blvd. Onsite parking available.

GPS Coordinates: 34.1639° N, 118.1664° W

Nearest Town: Pasadena

Interesting Facts: Starting in 1979 as a museum without walls, Kidspace now leads interactive learning with unique exhibits like the Hawk's Nest and Imagination Workshop.

Pasadena Playhouse

Why You Should Visit: The Pasadena Playhouse brings the vibrancy of live theater to life as the State Theater of California. This historic venue hosts an array of performances from musicals to dramas to groundbreaking new works. Its rich design paired with storytelling makes it a cultural Pasadena treasure.

Best Time to Visit: Year-round, check current schedule for performances.

Location: 39 S El Molino Ave, Pasadena, CA 91101

Directions: Near Colorado Blvd and El Molino Ave, a short drive from the 210 freeway exiting at Lake Ave south to Colorado Blvd west.

GPS Coordinates: 34.1455° N, 118.1374° W

Nearest Town: Pasadena

Interesting Facts: Established in 1917 with a rich history of iconic plays and acting careers launched, the Playhouse testifies to California's enduring performing arts love.

REDWOOD NATIONAL AND STATE PARKS

Tall Trees Grove

Why You Should Visit: Venturing into Tall Trees Grove feels like stepping back in time to an era of supreme nature. Towering redwoods, some over 350 feet tall, inspire awe and profound appreciation of the natural world. Strolling amid these ancient silent giants is a tranquil, humbling experience.

Best Time to Visit: May to October when weather is pleasant.

Location: Redwood National and State Parks, California.

Directions: Access requires permit from park visitor centers. Drive to Tall Trees Access Road, then hike down Tall Trees Trail.

GPS Coordinates: 41.2140° N, 124.0046° W

Nearest Town: Orick

Interesting Facts: Formerly home to the world's tallest tree, the serene, less trafficked grove allows experiencing pristine old growth redwoods.

Fern Canyon

Why You Should Visit: Fern Canyon is a surreal, verdant paradise where lush fern walls create a living, breathing fairy tale corridor. With its primeval ambiance, it has captured Hollywood's eye, serving as a "Jurassic Park" filming location.

Best Time to Visit: June to September.

Location: Prairie Creek Redwoods State Park, California.

Directions: From Orick, take the unpaved Davidson Road through Elk Prairie Campground to the trailhead parking lot.

GPS Coordinates: 41.4032° N, 124.0652° W

Nearest Town: Orick

Interesting Facts: Fern Canyon's awe-inspiring walls are ancient, with some species dating over 325 million years old, offering a glimpse of Earth's prehistoric past.

Lady Bird Johnson Grove

Why You Should Visit: Lady Bird Johnson Grove is a tranquil, majestic tribute to the former First Lady's conservation efforts. Wander amongst towering ancient redwoods, enveloped in the serene beauty and peace defining Redwood National Park. A breath of fresh air, the gentle trail winds through one of the park's loveliest old-growth forests.

Best Time to Visit: May to October.

Location: Redwood National and State Parks, California.

Directions: Located off Bald Hills Road, about 2 miles from Highway 101. Trailhead parking is well-marked.

GPS Coordinates: 41.3642° N, 124.0314° W

Nearest Town: Orick

Interesting Facts: Dedicated in 1969 by President Nixon, the grove celebrates Lady Bird Johnson's dedication to conservation and national beautification projects.

Prairie Creek Visitor Center

Why You Should Visit: Prairie Creek Visitor Center is the heart of the park, offering invaluable redwoods and ecosystem info. Get maps, learn about trails, wildlife, and history from knowledgeable rangers to start your ancient forest exploration.

Best Time to Visit: May to October.

Location: Prairie Creek Redwoods State Park, California.

Directions: Located on Newton B. Drury Scenic Parkway, a beautiful drive through towering redwoods. Straightforward from towns of Orick or Klamath.

GPS Coordinates: 41.4022° N, 124.0292° W

Nearest Town: Orick

Interesting Facts: Home to the World's Tallest Living Things, ancient coast redwoods, the park's rich biodiversity including Roosevelt elk herds makes the visitor center a gateway to understanding this habitat.

Enderts Beach

Why You Should Visit: Nestled within Redwood National and State Parks, pristine Enderts Beach offers tranquil coastal escape. Known for tide pools rich in marine life, its secluded nature provides peaceful seaside retreat amid stunning scenery. The adjacent coastal trail boasts splendid Pacific views, making it great for relaxation and exploration.

Best Time to Visit: June to September.

Location: Crescent City, CA 95531

Directions: Accessible via Enderts Beach Rd off Highway 101 south of Crescent City. Follow to parking, then a short trail to the beach.

GPS Coordinates: 41.7569° N, 124.1516° W

Nearest Town: Crescent City

Interesting Facts: Part of the Redwood parks preserving some of the world's last old-growth temperate rainforests, Enderts Beach is within a protected area spanning over 40 miles of rugged coastline and diverse ecosystems.

SACRAMENTO

California State Capitol Museum

(14)

Why You Should Visit: The California State Capitol Museum encapsulates the state's rich historical and political essence while standing as a living monument to the past. Nestled in a park, explore the historic Capitol, appreciate the legislative process, and delve into art and exhibits. Blending education with inspiration, it's a cornerstone for understanding California's heritage.

Best Time to Visit: Year-round.

Location: 1315 10th St, Sacramento, CA 95814

Directions: Located downtown, accessible by car with nearby parking or by light rail and bus transit.

GPS Coordinates: 38.5767° N, 121.4935° W

Nearest Town: Sacramento

Interesting Facts: The 1874 Capitol building is inspired by the U.S. Capitol. The museum offers a real-time glimpse into California's government in action.

Old Sacramento Waterfront District

Why You Should Visit: Step back in time strolling Old Sacramento's well-preserved Gold Rush-era buildings, wooden sidewalks, and charming horse carriages. The bustling riverfront, shops, museums, and eateries blend history, culture and modern enjoyment into a vibrant experience.

Best Time to Visit: March to October.

Location: 1002 2nd St, Sacramento, CA 95814

Directions: Near the American and Sacramento River confluence, accessible by car with nearby parking or transit.

GPS Coordinates: 38.5845° N, 121.5042° W

Nearest Town: Sacramento

Interesting Facts: Spanning 28 acres with over 50 historic buildings, the 1965 National Historic Landmark district continues as a hub of festivities and events, reflecting California's pioneering spirit.

California State Railroad Museum

Why You Should Visit: The Railroad Museum provides an exhilarating railway heritage journey, showcasing how iron horses significantly contributed to California's development. With restored locomotives, engaging exhibits and historic train rides, it thrills train aficionados and casual visitors alike in exploring this legacy.

Best Time to Visit: April to October.

Location: 125 I St, Sacramento, CA 95814

Directions: In Old Sacramento, accessible by car or transit with nearby parking.

GPS Coordinates: 38.5849° N, 121.5043° W

Nearest Town: Sacramento

Interesting Facts: With one of North America's most comprehensive railroad artifact collections, the museum's scholarly "Railroad History" journal has garnered acclaim, affirming its educational and historical significance.

Sacramento Zoo

Why You Should Visit: Sacramento Zoo offers a delightful family and wildlife outing with diverse animals. From colorful birds to majestic big cats and intriguing reptiles, it educates about conservation while providing interactive fun.

Best Time to Visit: March to May.

Location: 3930 W Land Park Dr, Sacramento, CA 95822

Directions: In William Land Park, accessible by car or public bus from downtown.

GPS Coordinates: 38.5393° N, 121.5030° W

Nearest Town: Sacramento

Interesting Facts: A cherished community treasure since 1927, the zoo has evolved to focus not just on an enjoyable visitor experience but also on conservation efforts and inspiring environmental care.

Sutter's Fort State Historic Park

Why You Should Visit: Sutter's Fort feels like time travel to the California Gold Rush era. The meticulously restored fort vividly depicts early Sacramento settlement life through educational, interactive experiences engaging all ages.

Best Time to Visit: September to May.

Location: 2701 L St, Sacramento, CA 95816

Directions: In downtown Sacramento, accessible by car or transit with nearby parking. A short drive from other attractions.

GPS Coordinates: 38.5727° N, 121.4710° W

Nearest Town: Sacramento

Interesting Facts: Established in 1839 by Swiss immigrant John Sutter, Sutter's Fort was the earliest non-Indigenous Central Valley community and played a crucial Gold Rush role. Now a National Historic Landmark, it offers insight into California's formative years.

SAN DIEGO

Balboa Park

Why You Should Visit: Balboa Park is San Diego's crown jewel of culture, with stunning museums, gardens, and the world-famous San Diego Zoo. Architectural magnificence paired with an extensive repertoire of exhibits offers a diversified, enriching cultural experience.

Best Time to Visit: March to May.

Location: 1549 El Prado, San Diego, CA 92101

Directions: Near downtown, accessible by car, bus, or taxi from the city center. Numerous parking lots available.

GPS Coordinates: 32.7314° N, 117.1516° W

Nearest Town: San Diego

Interesting Facts: Named after explorer Vasco Núñez de Balboa, Balboa Park is a testament to San Diego's maritime heritage. With 17 museums, venues, and 1,200 acres of gardens, it's one of the US's largest cultural complexes.

San Diego Zoo

Why You Should Visit: Nestled in Balboa Park, the San Diego Zoo is a haven for animal lovers. With over 3,700 animals representing 650+ species in cage-free, natural habitats, it offers thrilling glimpses of creatures from around the globe. Get up close with wildlife from every corner of the world.

Best Time to Visit: September to December.

Location: 2920 Zoo Dr, San Diego, CA 92101

Directions: In Balboa Park, accessible by car with ample parking or by public transit.

GPS Coordinates: 32.7353° N, 117.1510° W

Nearest Town: San Diego

Interesting Facts: A pioneer of cage-free, natural habitats, the San Diego Zoo is one of few zoos to have successfully bred endangered giant pandas, contributing significantly to conservation.

USS Midway Museum

Why You Should Visit: Anchored in San Diego Bay, the USS Midway Museum honors America's naval heritage. This historic aircraft carrier museum houses an extensive collection of interactive aircraft. Explore the engine room to flight deck for a sailor's life at sea glimpse.

Best Time to Visit: September to May.

Location: 910 N Harbor Dr, San Diego, CA 92101

Directions: Located downtown on Harbor Drive, accessible by car or transit with nearby parking.

GPS Coordinates: 32.7137° N, 117.1751° W

Nearest Town: San Diego

Interesting Facts: The longest-serving 20th century aircraft carrier, the USS Midway is now a floating city and freedom symbol. Its naval aviation collection from WWII through the jet age offers unique education.

La Jolla Cove

Why You Should Visit: La Jolla Cove is a picturesque small cove and beach nestled between sandstone cliffs. Part of an ecological reserve, it's excellent for snorkeling, diving, and observing seals and sea lions. Abundant marine life and dramatic cliffs provide a magical coastal escape.

Best Time to Visit: July to October.

Location: 1100 Coast Blvd, La Jolla, CA 92037

Directions: In La Jolla, a short drive from downtown San Diego, accessible by car with street parking.

GPS Coordinates: 32.8508° N, 117.2700° W

Nearest Town: La Jolla

Interesting Facts: One of San Diego's most photographed beaches for its stunning emerald waters and resident seals and sea lions, La Jolla Cove is part of a protected marine reserve, helping preserve the area's beauty and wildlife.

Old Town San Diego State Historic Park

Why You Should Visit: Old Town San Diego State Historic Park is a journey back to 1820s-1870s California. This protected park recreates and preserves San Diego's historic heart through original and reconstructed buildings. Costumed interpreters, crafts, and unique shops/restaurants create an interactive early California experience.

Best Time to Visit: September to November.

Location: 4002 Wallace St, San Diego, CA 92110

Directions: Near the I-5 and I-8 interchange. Take the Old Town exit off I-5, follow signs to the park. Free lot and street parking nearby.

GPS Coordinates: 32.7542° N, 117.1961° W

Nearest Town: San Diego

Interesting Facts: Considered California's "birthplace" as the site of the first permanent Spanish settlement, the park mixes authentic and reconstructed buildings including California's first schoolhouse, newspaper office, and historic homes.

SAN FRANCISCO

Golden Gate Bridge

(15)

Why You Should Visit: The Golden Gate Bridge is an iconic San Francisco emblem with a majestic structure spanning the Golden Gate Strait. Its distinctive "International Orange" color against the blue water and sky is a breathtaking sight. Walking across or viewing it from around the city offers unique, awe-inspiring experiences.

Best Time to Visit: September to November.

Location: Golden Gate Bridge, San Francisco, CA 94129

Directions: Easily accessible from US-101 North or South. Parking areas at both ends tend to fill fast.

GPS Coordinates: 37.8199° N, 122.4783° W

Nearest Town: San Francisco

Interesting Facts: The world's longest suspension bridge when completed in 1937, the Golden Gate Bridge is now one of the most photographed and recognized bridges globally. Its visible "International Orange" color was specifically chosen to enhance visibility in San Francisco's frequent fog.

Alcatraz Island

Why You Should Visit: Alcatraz Island holds a rich history as a former federal prison housing notorious inmates like Al Capone. Now a National Historic Landmark, the island beckons with eerie allure. Self-guided tours through cells narrated by former inmates/guards offer a chilling glimpse of life on "The Rock."

Best Time to Visit: September to November.

Location: Alcatraz Island, San Francisco, CA 94133

Directions: Access via ferry from Pier 33 Alcatraz Landing on the Embarcadero.

GPS Coordinates: 37.8267° N, 122.4230° W

Nearest Town: San Francisco

Interesting Facts: Alcatraz was considered America's safest, most secure prison due to its isolated location and the chilly, swift currents surrounding it - despite amenities like hot showers designed to deter escape attempts.

Fisherman's Wharf

Why You Should Visit: Fisherman's Wharf epitomizes San Francisco's vibrant waterfront culture, brimming with ships, seafood stalls and bustling markets. Maritime past and playful sea lions intertwine in this delightful melange. Take in the aroma of clam chowder as you explore the myriad shops, museums and scenic Bay vistas.

Best Time to Visit: September to November.

Location: Fisherman's Wharf, San Francisco, CA 94133

Directions: Accessible via cable cars, buses, streetcars. If driving, numerous nearby parking garages.

GPS Coordinates: 37.8080° N, 122.4177° W

Nearest Town: San Francisco

Interesting Facts: Home to the historic fleet of the National Maritime Park and famed Pier 39 sea lions, Fisherman's Wharf keeps its rich seafaring tradition alive with active fishermen and crabbers working in San Francisco's storied, oldest fishing district.

Chinatown

Why You Should Visit: San Francisco's Chinatown is the oldest in North America and largest Chinese community outside Asia. This bustling enclave transports you to Chinese American culture. Wander historic streets with apothecaries, teahouses and dragon-adorned temples mingling with modern eateries and boutiques.

Best Time to Visit: September to November.

Location: Grant Avenue and Stockton Street, San Francisco, CA 94108

Directions: In the city heart, accessible via Muni buses and cable cars. Nearby parking garages can fill fast.

GPS Coordinates: 37.7941° N, 122.4078° W

Nearest Town: San Francisco

Interesting Facts: More than a tourist destination, Chinatown is a living community with thousands of residents. Its distinct culture shines through festivals, particularly the elaborate Chinese New Year celebrations.

Lombard Street

Why You Should Visit: Known as the "crookedest street in the world," Lombard Street amazes with its sharp curves and stunning flowerbeds. This quirky, hilly street offers a fun, unique driving experience. Besides the zigzagging adventure, it provides spectacular city and bay views, making it a picturesque spot for photography.

Best Time to Visit: September to November.

Location: Lombard Street, between Jones and Hyde Streets, San Francisco, CA 94133

Directions: Reachable via the Powell-Hyde cable car line or by car, although parking is challenging.

GPS Coordinates: 37.8024° N, 122.4186° W

Nearest Town: San Francisco

Interesting Facts: The steep, one-block section with eight hairpin turns was engineered to reduce the natural steep slope - a marvel of design and San Francisco's hilly terrain.

SAN JOSE

The Tech Interactive

Why You Should Visit: The Tech Interactive is a shrine to innovation offering hands-on exploration of technology and science. This engaging hub fuels curiosity as visitors of all ages delve into interactive exhibits on topics from the internet to space. It celebrates human ingenuity in a compelling, interactive venue.

Best Time to Visit: September to May.

Location: 201 S Market St, San Jose, CA 95113

Directions: Located downtown with nearby parking and transit like VTA Light Rail.

GPS Coordinates: 37.3307° N, 121.8907° W

Nearest Town: San Jose

Interesting Facts: Recognized as a science education leader and multi-award winner, The Tech makes learning captivating by fusing exploration and education.

Winchester Mystery House

Why You Should Visit: The Winchester Mystery House offers a quirky, fascinating dive into the peculiar. Once home to Sarah Winchester, this architectural marvel is famous for bizarre choices like staircases to nowhere. It's a unique blend of eerie yet elegant, enveloping you in mystery and opulence from a bygone era.

Best Time to Visit: April to July.

Location: 525 S Winchester Blvd, San Jose, CA 95128

Directions: Near Santana Row, accessible via I-280 or I-880. VTA buses stop nearby.

GPS Coordinates: 37.3184° N, 121.9509° W

Nearest Town: San Jose

Interesting Facts: With 160 rooms, 2,000 doors, 47 fireplaces and 40 staircases, the Mystery House's enigmatic design is said to evade spirits of those killed by Winchester rifles, offering perplexing yet intriguing insight into its reclusive inhabitant's mind.

Rosicrucian Egyptian Museum

Why You Should Visit: The Rosicrucian Egyptian Museum is a gateway to ancient Egypt in San Jose's heart. It boasts the largest exhibit of Egyptian artifacts in western North America. Immersive experiences like a rock-cut tomb replica transport you back to the age of pharaohs.

Best Time to Visit: March to May.

Location: 1660 Park Ave, San Jose, CA 95191

Directions: Near Rose Garden, accessible by car or transit with nearby bus stops.

GPS Coordinates: 37.3345° N, 121.9225° W

Nearest Town: San Jose

Interesting Facts: Along with over 4,000 artifacts, the museum houses mummies, stelae, and daily life objects, offering comprehensive insight into ancient Egyptian life and culture.

San Jose Museum of Art

Why You Should Visit: The San Jose Museum of Art is a vibrant modern and contemporary art hub, displaying diverse works reflecting Silicon Valley's innovative spirit. The collection includes significant 20th and 21st century pieces in various mediums like painting, sculpture, photography and digital media.

Best Time to Visit: March to May.

Location: 110 S Market St, downtown San Jose

Directions: Easily accessible by car or transit, with nearby parking and bus stops. The Convention Center light rail station is close by.

GPS Coordinates: 37.3337° N, 121.8902° W

Nearest Town: San Jose

Interesting Facts: The museum blends old and new with a historic 20th century wing and modern addition, symbolizing the marriage of history and contemporary art.

Happy Hollow Park & Zoo

Why You Should Visit: Happy Hollow Park & Zoo blends wildlife education and playful amusement into a delightful family spot. Meet animals from across the globe, enjoy rides and puppet shows for a fun, educational outing.

Best Time to Visit: March to May.

Location: 748 Story Rd, San Jose

Directions: In central San Jose, easily accessible by car with onsite parking. Also reachable by VTA bus.

GPS Coordinates: 37.3256° N, 121.8616° W

Nearest Town: San Jose

Interesting Facts: Open since 1961, Happy Hollow holds a special community place. It is dedicated to conservation and fostering meaningful connections between visitors and nature.

SANTA BARBARA

Santa Barbara Mission

Why You Should Visit: The "Queen of the Missions," Santa Barbara Mission offers a glimpse into California's rich history and culture. Striking architecture, lush gardens, and an informative museum provide a peaceful retreat and journey through the state's colonial era.

Best Time to Visit: March to May.

Location: 2201 Laguna St, Santa Barbara, CA 93105

Directions: A short drive from downtown, accessible by car or transit like the local buses.

GPS Coordinates: 34.4383° N, 119.7145° W

Nearest Town: Santa Barbara

Interesting Facts: Founded in 1786 as the tenth of California's 21 Spanish Franciscan missions, Santa Barbara is known for its iconic twin bell towers and continues as a living friary today.

Santa Barbara Zoo

Why You Should Visit: The Santa Barbara Zoo provides an intimate, charming setting to admire 500+ animals across 146 species. With sprawling lawns, Pacific views, and interactive exhibits, it's a delightful haven for families and wildlife enthusiasts.

Best Time to Visit: Year-round.

Location: 500 Ninos Dr, Santa Barbara, CA 93103

Directions: Near East Beach, accessible by car or local transit buses.

GPS Coordinates: 34.4194° N, 119.6587° W

Nearest Town: Santa Barbara

Interesting Facts: Recognized for its personal atmosphere and conservation education, the Santa Barbara Zoo was home to Sujatha the Asian elephant, who lived to 47, marking a major milestone for captive elephants.

Lotusland

Why You Should Visit: In Montecito, Lotusland is a 37-acre botanical haven filled with unique exotic plants. Created by opera singer Ganna Walska, it hosts surreal themed gardens that engage the senses and spark imagination, like the cycad, cactus and signature water lotus gardens.

Best Time to Visit: February to November.

Location: Cold Springs Road, Montecito, CA 93108

Directions: Reservations required for this residential area, with exact address provided when booked.

GPS Coordinates: 34.4339° N, 119.6506° W

Nearest Town: Montecito

Interesting Facts: Beginning in 1941 when purchased by Ganna Walska, she transformed it over the years into a mesmerizing botanical garden and living art providing an inspiring, educational experience.

Santa Barbara Museum of Art

Why You Should Visit: The Santa Barbara Museum of Art is a treasure trove of over 27,000 works spanning 5,000 years of creativity. It houses impressive American, European, and Asian art for a diverse artistic experience. As a hub of cultural enrichment, it is also committed to education and community engagement.

Best Time to Visit: Year-round.

Location: 1130 State St, downtown Santa Barbara

Directions: A short drive from Highway 101, exiting at Carrillo St to State St. Also accessible by public transit.

GPS Coordinates: 34.4250° N, 119.7070° W

Nearest Town: Santa Barbara

Interesting Facts: Housed in a historic 1930s post office, the museum is renowned for its Monet collection and blend of Western and Eastern art.

El Capitan State Beach

Why You Should Visit: El Capitan State Beach is a picturesque California coast jewel with rocky tide pools, sandy coves, and rugged cliff backdrops. A haven for hiking, camping, swimming, and wildlife spotting.

Best Time to Visit: May to October.

Location: Off Highway 101, 17 miles west of Santa Barbara.

Directions: Exit Highway 101 at El Capitan State Beach Road, follow it a short distance to the beach.

GPS Coordinates: 34.4609° N, 120.0719° W

Nearest Town: Goleta

Interesting Facts: Named after the Spanish military term for "The Captain," El Capitan State Beach offers serene settings with sycamore and oak trees shading the campgrounds.

Natural Bridges State Beach

Why You Should Visit: Natural Bridges State Beach is famed for its stunning rock formations carved by water. Serene beach, tide pools, and seasonal monarch migrations offer tranquil yet engaging experiences. It's a coastal paradise where nature's artistry shines.

Best Time to Visit: October-February for monarch migrations, otherwise May-September for warm weather.

Location: 2531 W Cliff Dr, Santa Cruz, CA

Directions: From Santa Cruz center go northwest on Mission St/CA-1, turn right on Swift St, left on W Cliff Dr.

GPS Coordinates: 36.9529° N, 122.0577° W

Nearest Town: Santa Cruz

Interesting Facts: Named for its natural stone bridges, though only one remains today. The Monarch Butterfly Natural Preserve is winter home to 100,000+ monarchs.

Mystery Spot

Why You Should Visit: The Mystery Spot is a gravitational anomaly in the California redwoods near Santa Cruz. Within a 150-foot circular area, you'll experience phenomena defying gravity and perception. The tilted environment, height anomalies, and visual contradictions make for a fun, mind-boggling excursion challenging physics and sparking curiosity.

Best Time to Visit: March to November.

Location: 465 Mystery Spot Rd, Santa Cruz, CA

Directions: From Santa Cruz, take Branciforte Dr north to Glen Canyon Rd. Turn right, then left onto Mystery Spot Rd.

GPS Coordinates: 37.0167° N, 122.0024° W

Nearest Town: Santa Cruz

Interesting Facts: Discovered in 1939 and opened in 1940, the cause of the Mystery Spot's gravitational anomaly remains unknown, adding to its allure.

Santa Cruz Wharf

Why You Should Visit: Santa Cruz Wharf, extending into Monterey Bay's cool waters, is an iconic city landmark. Its rustic charm and Pacific views invite exploring dining, shopping, and recreation. Blending historical elegance, soothing waves, and lounging sea lions crafts a unique coastal experience that's quintessentially Californian.

Best Time to Visit: June to August.

Location: 21 Municipal Wharf, Santa Cruz, CA

Directions: Head southwest on Pacific Ave, right on Beach St, left onto Municipal Wharf.

GPS Coordinates: 36.9586° N, 122.0171° W

Nearest Town: Santa Cruz

Interesting Facts: One of the West Coast's longest at 2,745 feet, the Santa Cruz Wharf has stood since 1914 as a living testament to the region's maritime history.

Seymour Marine Discovery Center

Why You Should Visit: The Seymour Marine Discovery Center is a doorway to Monterey Bay's watery world, where marine life wonders unfold before your eyes. Interactive exhibits, touch tanks, and the iconic 87-foot Ms. Blue whale skeleton offer intimate Pacific biodiversity encounters that nurture ocean appreciation.

Best Time to Visit: April to September.

Location: 100 McAllister Way, Santa Cruz, CA

Directions: From downtown Santa Cruz, head northwest on Mission St/CA-1, turn right on Western Dr, left on McAllister Way.

GPS Coordinates: 36.9510° N, 122.0644° W

Nearest Town: Santa Cruz

Interesting Facts: Part of UC Santa Cruz's Long Marine Lab, the center offers a glimpse into ongoing marine research and conservation efforts. Ms. Blue gives tangible scale to the ocean's magnificent creatures.

SANTA MONICA

Santa Monica Pier

(16)

Why You Should Visit: The Santa Monica Pier is a classic Californian landmark embodying the west coast's free spirit. Historic carousel, family aquarium, and the endearing end of Route 66 blend timeless charm with the Pacific's playful allure. Wandering the bustling boardwalk, street performers and amusement park capture the essence of seaside merriment.

Best Time to Visit: May to October.

Location: 200 Santa Monica Pier, Santa Monica, CA 90401

Directions: From downtown L.A., take I-10 W to exit 1A onto 4th St, Santa Monica.

GPS Coordinates: 34.0094° N, 118.4973° W

Nearest Town: Santa Monica

Interesting Facts: The pier's solar-paneled Ferris wheel in Pacific Park is the world's only solar-powered Ferris wheel, showcasing eco-conscious spirit.

Third Street Promenade

Why You Should Visit: For lively, eclectic shopping, Santa Monica's Third Street Promenade is a go-to destination. This open-air district brims with trendy boutiques to retail giants catering to diverse tastes. Strolling through, street musicians' tunes add whimsical charm to your spree. The blend of shopping, dining and entertainment amid palm-lined streets captures Santa Monica's vibrant ethos.

Best Time to Visit: Year-round.

Location: 3rd Street Promenade, Santa Monica, CA 90401

Directions: From the pier, head northeast on Colorado Ave, left on 2nd St, left on Santa Monica Blvd, right on 3rd St.

GPS Coordinates: 34.0162° N, 118.4965° W

Nearest Town: Santa Monica

Interesting Facts: Beyond shopping, the Promenade is a cultural hub hosting year-round events and performances that embody Santa Monica's vibrant arts scene.

Santa Monica State Beach

Why You Should Visit: Santa Monica State Beach embodies SoCal's laid-back beach culture with vast sandy shores perfect for sunbathing, volleyball, or people watching. The iconic pier offers classic fun with its amusement park, aquarium, and family restaurants. Serene sunsets, crashing waves, and the Ferris wheel silhouette against the evening sky create a poetic urban retreat.

Best Time to Visit: May to October.

Location: Pacific Coast Hwy, Santa Monica, CA 90401

Directions: From downtown L.A., take I-10 W, exit on Lincoln Blvd, right on Pico Blvd.

GPS Coordinates: 34.0104° N, 118.4962° W

Nearest Town: Santa Monica

Interesting Facts: Famous for its iconinc pier with Pacific Park, historic Looff Carousel, and interactive aquarium.

Palisades Park

Why You Should Visit: Perched on bluffs overlooking the Pacific, Palisades Park offers tranquil escape in bustling Santa Monica. Meticulous walking paths, inviting benches, and sculptures/memorials make it great for strolls, jogs, or soaking up stunning ocean views. With its rose garden, historic pergola, and palms, its serene ambiance is perfect for relaxing, reflecting, or picnicking.

Best Time to Visit: March-June, September-November.

Location: Ocean Ave, Santa Monica, CA 90401

Directions: From the pier, head north on Ocean Ave. Street parking available.

GPS Coordinates: 34.0224° N, 118.5015° W

Nearest Town: Santa Monica

Interesting Facts: One of Santa Monica's oldest parks, Palisades Park hosts historic landmarks and prime sunset viewing over the Pacific.

Santa Monica Mountains National Recreation Area

Why You Should Visit: The Santa Monica Mountains Recreation Area unfolds as rugged mountains, verdant valleys, and picturesque coast - nature's escape in L.A.'s backyard. Explore over 500 miles of trails, diverse flora and fauna, and rich cultural history. Sweeping mountain vistas and tranquil beaches provide refreshing contrast to urban sprawl.

Best Time to Visit: October to May.

Location: 26876 Mulholland Hwy, Calabasas, CA 91302

Directions: From downtown L.A. take US-101 N, exit 29 to Valley Cir Blvd, follow to Visitor Center.

GPS Coordinates: 34.1155° N, 118.7569° W

Nearest Town: Calabasas

Interesting Facts: The world's largest urban national park, it's home to the iconic 67-mile Backbone Trail, offering thorough exploration of the diverse landscapes.

SEQUOIA AND KINGS CANYON NATIONAL PARKS

General Sherman Tree

Why You Should Visit: The General Sherman Tree in Sequoia National Park is the largest living tree on earth by volume, testifying to the ancient world's majestic grandeur. Its staggering dimensions embody the giant sequoias, making it a must-see natural wonder. The easy trail lined with other giants leads to quietly standing in awe at the base of this colossal tree.

Best Time to Visit: June to August.

Location: Sequoia National Park, California

Directions: From Foothills Visitor Center, drive 16 miles on Generals Highway to the Sherman Tree parking area. Shuttles also available in summer.

GPS Coordinates: 36.5802° N, 118.7496° W

Nearest Town: Three Rivers

Interesting Facts: At 275 feet tall, 102 feet around, and estimated to be 2,200 years old, the General Sherman Tree showcases a fascinating intertwine of longevity and grandiosity.

Moro Rock

Why You Should Visit: Moro Rock's granite dome offers a steep stair-climbed trail to panoramic vistas of the Great Western Divide and Sequoia National Park's vastness. The exhilarating journey rewards those who ascend with a sense of adventure and awe-inspiring views.

Best Time to Visit: May to October.

Location: Sequoia National Park, California

Directions: From Foothills Visitor Center, drive an hour on Generals Highway to Giant Forest Museum, then take Moro Rock/Crescent Meadow Road.

GPS Coordinates: 36.5450° N, 118.7654° W

Nearest Town: Three Rivers

Interesting Facts: The 6,725-foot summit staircase was constructed in the 1930s, showcasing early park infrastructure development for intimate landscape experiences.

Crystal Cave

Why You Should Visit: Crystal Cave is a mineral marvel deep within Sequoia National Park. Adorned with stalactites, stalagmites, and whimsical formations, this marble cave offers surreal underground adventure. Guided tours provide insights into the delicate ecosystem and geologic forces, enriching your wonder.

Best Time to Visit: May to September.

Location: Sequoia National Park, California

Directions: From Foothills Visitor Center, drive along Generals Highway and follow Crystal Cave Road signs. Access is by guided tour only with advance ticket purchase.

GPS Coordinates: 36.5547° N, 118.7490° W

Nearest Town: Three Rivers

Interesting Facts: Discovered in 1918, Crystal Cave is one of over 200 caves in Sequoia and Kings Canyon Parks. Its year-round 48°F temperature provides cool summer respite.

Zumwalt Meadow

Why You Should Visit: Zumwalt Meadow provides serene escape amid Kings Canyon's cliffs and lush greenery. The gentle trail winds through diverse landscapes from verdant meadows to tranquil river scenes and imposing granite. Here the park's grandeur condenses into an accessible, picturesque setting.

Best Time to Visit: June to September.

Location: Kings Canyon National Park, California

Directions: Take Highway 180 into the park. Continue to the well-signed Zumwalt Meadow trailhead parking.

GPS Coordinates: 36.7942° N, 118.5839° W

Nearest Town: Fresno

Interesting Facts: Named for an early 20th century superintendent who promoted the park, the relatively flat, easy Zumwalt Meadow trail provides accessible glimpses into the park's diverse ecosystems and geologic wonders.

Roaring River Falls

Why You Should Visit: Roaring River Falls is a thunderous cascade nestled in Kings Canyon's wilderness. The dramatic falls crash into a serene pool below, surrounded by rugged rocks and lush greenery, displaying nature's power. It's a short, easy hike to the viewpoint, making it a quick yet rewarding park stop.

Best Time to Visit: May to September.

Location: Kings Canyon National Park, California

Directions: From the Big Stump entrance on Highway 180 east, turn right to the Roaring River Falls parking lot after entering the park.

GPS Coordinates: 36.7940° N, 118.6028° W

Nearest Town: Fresno

Interesting Facts: One of Kings Canyon's most accessible waterfalls, the short hike and dramatic cascade make Roaring River Falls a popular stop to experience the park's beauty with minimal effort.

SOLVANG

Solvang Village

Why You Should Visit: Quaint Solvang Village sweeps you into a Danish fairy tale in California's heart. With authentic architecture, windmills, bakeries, boutiques and cozy eateries, it provides a unique European experience. Stroll leisurely, shop for European goods, and indulge in Danish pastries.

Best Time to Visit: March to May.

Location: Solvang, California

Directions: Off US Highway 101 in the Santa Ynez Valley, about 35 miles north of Santa Barbara. Exit onto CA-246 east.

GPS Coordinates: 34.5958° N, 120.1376° W

Nearest Town: Santa Barbara

Interesting Facts: Founded in 1911 by Danes escaping Midwest winters, Solvang remains a vibrant Danish cultural link known as the "Danish Capital of America" with traditional architecture and festivities.

Hans Christian Andersen Museum

Why You Should Visit: This cozy museum above The Book Loft pays tribute to prolific fairy tale author Hans Christian Andersen. Filled with memorabilia, books, and displays, it offers a glimpse into Andersen's whimsical world, making you part of tales like "The Little Mermaid."

Best Time to Visit: March to May.

Location: 1680 Mission Dr, Solvang, CA 93463

Directions: Located downtown on Mission Drive, accessible by car with nearby street parking.

GPS Coordinates: 34.5950° N, 120.1407° W

Nearest Town: Santa Barbara

Interesting Facts: Operated by the non-profit Ugly Duckling Foundation, the museum is dedicated to preserving and expanding understanding of Andersen's work as a free cultural resource.

Old Mission Santa Ines

Why You Should Visit: In Solvang's heart, Old Mission Santa Ines captures California's multi-cultural history through serene gardens and the sacred ambiance of its chapel and museum - a peaceful, enriching blend. With authentic architecture and valley views, the Mission bridges to California's past, making it a serene and enlightening spot.

Best Time to Visit: March to May.

Location: 1760 Mission Dr, Solvang, CA 93463

Directions: On Mission Drive, easily accessible from Highway 101 by exiting at CA-246 east.

GPS Coordinates: 34.5958° N, 120.1376° W

Nearest Town: Solvang

Interesting Facts: Founded in 1804 as the 19th of 21 California Franciscan missions, it played a key early role in agricultural development.

Elverhoj Museum of History & Art

Why You Should Visit: The Elverhoj Museum tucked inside a charming Danish building remarkably embodies Solvang's roots. Engaging exhibits immerse you in the region's cultural and historical tapestry through local art, history, and Danish heritage. As you wander through quaint rooms, you're whisked on a journey melding old world Danish charm with Solvang's contemporary allure.

Best Time to Visit: Year-round.

Location: 1624 Elverhoy Way, Solvang, CA 93463

Directions: From Highway 101, exit CA-246 W, turn right on Alisal Rd, left on Elverhoy Way.

GPS Coordinates: 34.5959° N, 120.1420° W

Nearest Town: Solvang

Interesting Facts: Housed in a hand-crafted Danish-style building with notable hand-carved redwood façade, it captivates visually before even exploring the exhibits.

Sunny Fields Park

Why You Should Visit: Sunny Fields Park is a delightful slice of outdoor fun in Solvang, with a whimsical playground mirroring a miniature Danish village. Epitomizing Solvang's charm, it provides a space for kids and adults to relish the outdoors. The intricately designed playground, lush fields, and serene ambiance make it perfect for family picnics or leisurely afternoons.

Best Time to Visit: March-June, September-November for pleasant weather.

Location: 900 Alamo Pintado Rd, Solvang, CA 93463

Directions: From downtown, head north on Alisal Rd, right on Mission Dr, left on Alamo Pintado Rd.

GPS Coordinates: 34.6024° N, 120.1367° W

Nearest Town: Solvang

Interesting Facts: The Danish-themed structures like the windmill and buildings nod to Solvang's heritage, making the park a playful extension of the town's character.

TEMECULA

Temecula Valley Wine Country

(17)

Why You Should Visit: Temecula Valley Wine Country beckons oenophiles and casual wine lovers with picturesque vineyards and award-winning wines. Over 40 wineries offer a plethora of tasting experiences amid rolling hills and scenic landscapes - a delightful escape to savor fine wines, delicious fare, and peaceful countryside charm.

Best Time to Visit: September to November during grape harvest season.

Location: Temecula, CA

Directions: From Interstate 15, exit Rancho California Rd east, leading directly into the wine country.

GPS Coordinates: 33.4936° N, 117.1484° W

Nearest Town: Temecula

Interesting Facts: A prime Southern California wine region with history dating to the 18th century, Temecula Valley is especially known for its diverse wine varieties and welcoming family-owned wineries.

Old Town Temecula

Why You Should Visit: Old Town Temecula blends history and charm with modern boutiques, antique shops, and eateries housed in historic buildings. Wooden boardwalks and storefronts transport you to California's rustic past while offering contemporary experiences. Here, the state's early days are celebrated and cherished.

Best Time to Visit: October to June for pleasant weather and fewer crowds.

Location: Temecula, CA

Directions: Easily accessible from I-15 by exiting at Rancho California Rd or Temecula Pkwy and following signs.

GPS Coordinates: 33.4936° N, 117.1475° W

Nearest Town: Temecula

Interesting Facts: Home to landmarks like Temecula Stampede music venue and Old Temecula Community Theater, Old Town is a vibrant cultural hub hosting performances and events year-round.

Pechanga Casino

Why You Should Visit: Beyond a place to try your luck, Pechanga Resort Casino is a full entertainment destination as California's largest casino. It offers a dizzying array of gaming from slots to tables. The resort also features a luxurious spa, golf course, dining options, top-notch live acts, and special events adding excitement.

Best Time to Visit: Year-round, though weekends and events can be bustling.

Location: 45000 Pechanga Pkwy, Temecula, CA 92592

Directions: Easily accessible from I-15 by taking the Temecula Pkwy exit and following signs.

GPS Coordinates: 33.4648° N, 117.1103° W

Nearest Town: Temecula

Interesting Facts: Owned by the Pechanga Band of Luiseño Indians, the Resort and Casino contribute to the local economy and community through charitable initiatives, not just entertainment.

Temecula Valley Museum

Why You Should Visit: The Temecula Valley Museum provides a colorful glimpse into the region's past, making it a captivating history buff stop. Engaging exhibits narrate the area's development from indigenous roots to modern growth. Artifacts, photographs, and displays bring local heritage to life. It's a compact yet enriching museum to discover what shaped the valley.

Best Time to Visit: Year-round, weekends offer guided tours.

Location: 28314 Mercedes St, in Old Town Temecula

Directions: Accessible via I-15, exit Rancho California Rd east to Old Town.

GPS Coordinates: 33.4936° N, 117.1474° W

Nearest Town: Temecula

Interesting Facts: The museum also hosts community events and educational programs, making it a hub of Temecula Valley's cultural activity and an enjoyable way to learn local history.

Pennypickle's Workshop - Temecula Children's Museum

Why You Should Visit: Pennypickle's Workshop, or the Temecula Children's Museum, is a realm of imagination and exploration where science and fun meld playfully to spark curiosity and foster learning love. Interactive exhibits and hands-on activities encourage kids to touch, play, and discover mysteries. It's an enthralling adventure making learning exhilarating for kids and adults alike.

Best Time to Visit: Year-round, less crowded on weekdays.

Location: 42081 Main St, in Old Town Temecula

Directions: Accessible via I-15, exit Rancho California Rd east.

GPS Coordinates: 33.4930° N, 117.1476° W

Nearest Town: Temecula

Interesting Facts: Themed around fictional inventor Professor Pennypickle, his home is filled with quirky inventions making science an enchanting adventure.

YOSEMITE NATIONAL PARK

Yosemite Valley

(18)

Why You Should Visit: Yosemite Valley is Yosemite National Park's crown jewel, boasting awe-inspiring cliffs, waterfalls, and meadows. This glacial valley epitomizes nature's raw beauty and grandeur, with icons like El Capitan and Half Dome as silent sentinels over the serene landscape. The valley also serves as a gateway to wilderness hikes and adventures, offering a sublime escape into nature. Its breathtaking scenery and tranquility make it a haven for nature lovers, photographers, and anyone seeking respite.

Best Time to Visit: May to September has warm weather and accessible features.

Location: Yosemite National Park, California

Directions: Accessible via CA-41, CA-120 or CA-140. Follow signs to the valley once inside the park.

GPS Coordinates: 37.8651° N, 119.5383° W

Nearest Town: Mariposa

Interesting Facts: Though only 1% of the park area, most visitors spend time in Yosemite Valley for its iconic landmarks and amenities.

Half Dome

Why You Should Visit: Half Dome is one of Yosemite's most iconic formations, offering hikers a unique challenge and all visitors a picturesque view. This granite dome stands nearly 5,000 feet above the valley with panoramic vistas from its summit. The final ascent requires daring cable route climbing. Reaching the top is a rewarding achievement with an unparalleled Yosemite Valley and High Sierra view.

Best Time to Visit: Late May to early October when cables are up and weather permits hiking.

Location: Yosemite National Park, California

Directions: Trailhead located at Yosemite Valley's eastern end. Take shuttle or park at the lot.

GPS Coordinates: 37.7460° N, 119.5331° W

Nearest Town: Mariposa

Interesting Facts: Once deemed inaccessible, daring hikers can now summit Half Dome via cable routes to experience breathtaking views of Yosemite National Park.

El Capitan

Why You Should Visit: El Capitan is a majestic vertical rock formation in Yosemite, rising about 3,000 feet along its tallest granite face. This monolith magnetizes rock climbers from around the globe with challenging, exhilarating climbs. Even for non-climbers, El Capitan's sheer grandeur is a spectacle to behold.

Best Time to Visit: Late spring to early fall for warmer weather.

Location: Yosemite National Park, California

Directions: Visible from many Yosemite Valley viewpoints, especially El Capitan Meadow.

GPS Coordinates: 37.7341° N, 119.6373° W

Nearest Town: Mariposa

Interesting Facts: El Capitan's daunting Dawn Wall, free-climbed in 2015, is considered one of the world's most difficult.

Mariposa Grove of Giant Sequoias

Why You Should Visit: Home to 500+ mature giant sequoias, the Mariposa Grove is a living ancient world testament. These towering behemoths are the largest and oldest living things on Earth, some over 200 feet tall and 2,000 years old. Trails allow visitors to wander and soak in the tranquil forest beauty.

Best Time to Visit: May to October.

Location: Yosemite National Park, California

Directions: Near the South Entrance. Take the free shuttle from the Welcome Plaza.

GPS Coordinates: 37.5026° N, 119.6042° W

Nearest Town: Fish Camp

Interesting Facts: The Grizzly Giant tree is estimated to be 1,800-2,400 years old, making it one of the grove's oldest living entities.

Glacier Point

Why You Should Visit: Glacier Point offers an unparalleled Yosemite vista - the mesmerizing valley, Half Dome, and three waterfalls. This quintessential spot for photographers and nature lovers stands about 3,200 feet above the valley, providing breathtaking perspective on Yosemite's rugged beauty.

Best Time to Visit: May to November when Glacier Point Road is usually open.

Location: Yosemite National Park, California

Directions: Accessible by car, about a 30-45 minute drive from Yosemite Valley on Glacier Point Road.

GPS Coordinates: 37.7275° N, 119.5742° W

Nearest Town: Yosemite Valley

Interesting Facts: A major attraction since the 1870s, Glacier Point also provides a unique top-down view of Yosemite Valley, usually seen from the bottom up.

California Adventure:
2 Magic Itineraries Proposals

7-Day California Adventure: From South to North

Get ready for a week of illuminating explorations as we traverse the length of captivating California from south to north, uncovering a trove of alluring cities, breathtaking shores, and stunning landscapes. Follow this day-by-day guide that will lead you on an unforgettable voyage up the coast, inviting you to discover incredible urban energy, iconic beaches, misty redwood forests, and more as you experience the diverse beauty and culture that makes California so extraordinary.

Day 1: San Diego

- Morning: Arrive in San Diego and settle into your accommodation.

- Afternoon: Explore Balboa Park with its numerous museums and beautiful gardens.

- Evening: Dine in the Gaslamp Quarter and explore the vibrant nightlife.

Day 2: San Diego to Los Angeles

- Morning: Enjoy a hearty breakfast then hit the road to Los Angeles.

- Afternoon: Arrive in LA and visit the iconic Hollywood Walk of Fame.

- Evening: Explore Santa Monica Pier and enjoy dinner with a Pacific Ocean view.

Day 3: Los Angeles

- Morning: Visit Universal Studios Hollywood for a day of movie magic.

- Evening: Drive to Venice Beach for a relaxing sunset stroll.

Day 4: Los Angeles to Santa Barbara

- Morning: Depart for Santa Barbara. Stop by Malibu's beaches for a quick swim.

- Afternoon: Arrive in Santa Barbara. Explore the historic Mission Santa Barbara.

- Evening: Enjoy dinner downtown, tasting the local wine.

Day 5: Santa Barbara to San Francisco

- Morning: Hit the road early for a scenic drive along the Pacific Coast Highway.

- Afternoon: Stop at McWay Falls in Big Sur for photos.

- Evening: Arrive in San Francisco. Take a night stroll at Fisherman's Wharf.

Day 6: San Francisco

- Morning: Visit Alcatraz Island.

- Afternoon: Ride the cable cars and explore Lombard Street.

- Evening: Dine in Chinatown and explore the city's nightlife.

Day 7: San Francisco to Napa Valley

- Morning: Depart for Napa Valley.

- Afternoon: Enjoy wine tasting tours at local vineyards.

- Evening: Relax and dine at a countryside restaurant before heading back to San Francisco or staying overnight in Napa.

California Voyage: Northern Narratives

Continue unraveling Northern California's wonders, picking up where your Napa Valley adventures left off for seven more days of illuminating expeditions further north. This carefully planned itinerary will immerse you in the region's varied scenery, distinctive culture, and vibrant urban energy as you journey onward. It promises a smooth transition from previous explorations, inviting you to dive deeper into the diverse beauty and magnetism that makes Northern California such an unforgettable destination.

Day 8: Napa Valley to Sacramento

- Morning: Depart for Sacramento, the state's capital.

- Afternoon: Explore the historic Old Sacramento Waterfront and learn about California's Gold Rush era.

- Evening: Enjoy a dinner cruise on the Sacramento River.

Day 9: Sacramento to Lake Tahoe

- Morning: Hit the road early towards Lake Tahoe.

- Afternoon: Arrive at Lake Tahoe and indulge in some water activities or relax by the beach.

- Evening: Dine by the lake and enjoy the tranquil sunset.

Day 10: Lake Tahoe Exploration

- Morning: Explore Emerald Bay State Park and go for a hike to Eagle Falls.

- Afternoon: Take a scenic cruise around Lake Tahoe.

- Evening: Try your luck at one of the local casinos or enjoy a relaxing night at your accommodation.

Day 11: Lake Tahoe to Yosemite National Park

- Morning: Depart early for Yosemite National Park.

- Afternoon: Explore Yosemite Valley, visiting iconic spots like El Capitan and Yosemite Falls.

- Evening: Settle into your accommodation and prepare for a day of exploration tomorrow.

Day 12: Yosemite National Park

- Morning: Hike to the top of Vernal Fall and Nevada Fall along the Mist Trail.

- Afternoon: Drive to Glacier Point for breathtaking views of the park.

- Evening: Enjoy a campfire program at one of the park's campgrounds.

Day 13: Yosemite to Monterey

- Morning: Depart for Monterey.

- Afternoon: Arrive in Monterey and visit the famous Monterey Bay Aquarium.

- Evening: Stroll along Cannery Row and enjoy a seafood dinner.

Day 14: Monterey to Santa Cruz

- Morning: Take a scenic drive along 17-Mile Drive.

- Afternoon: Arrive in Santa Cruz and enjoy some fun at the Santa Cruz Beach Boardwalk.

- Evening: Relax on the beach or explore the downtown area for dinner and entertainment.

Travel

Journal Section

DATE OF VISIT: _____

NUMBER OF DAYS SPENT: _____

WEATHER CONDITIONS

WHAT I VISITED

WHAT I BOUGHT

WHERE I SLEPT

WHERE I EAT

WHO I MET

SECTION TO MARK THE SCORE FROM 0 TO 10

| 0 | 1 | 2 | 3 | 4 | 5 | 6 | 7 | 8 | 9 | 10 |

THE MOST BEAUTIFUL MEMORY

Travel

Journal Section

DATE OF VISIT: _____

NUMBER OF DAYS SPENT: _____

WEATHER CONDITIONS

_____
_____
_____
_____

WHAT I VISITED

_____
_____
_____
_____

WHAT I BOUGHT

WHERE I SLEPT

WHERE I EAT

_____
_____
_____
_____

WHO I MET

_____
_____
_____
_____

SECTION TO MARK THE SCORE FROM 0 TO 10

| 0 | 1 | 2 | 3 | 4 | 5 | 6 | 7 | 8 | 9 | 10 |

THE MOST BEAUTIFUL MEMORY

_____
_____
_____

Travel

Journal Section

DATE OF VISIT: ....

NUMBER OF DAYS SPENT: ....

WEATHER CONDITIONS

WHAT I VISITED

WHAT I BOUGHT

WHERE I SLEPT

WHERE I EAT

WHO I MET

SECTION TO MARK THE SCORE FROM 0 TO 10

| 0 | 1 | 2 | 3 | 4 | 5 | 6 | 7 | 8 | 9 | 10 |

THE MOST BEAUTIFUL MEMORY

Travel

Journal Section

DATE OF VISIT: _____

NUMBER OF DAYS SPENT: _____

WEATHER CONDITIONS

_____
_____
_____
_____

WHAT I VISITED

_____
_____
_____
_____

WHAT I BOUGHT

WHERE I SLEPT

WHERE I EAT

_____
_____
_____
_____

WHO I MET

_____
_____
_____
_____

SECTION TO MARK THE SCORE FROM 0 TO 10

| 0 | 1 | 2 | 3 | 4 | 5 | 6 | 7 | 8 | 9 | 10 |

THE MOST BEAUTIFUL MEMORY

_____
_____
_____

Travel

Journal Section

DATE OF VISIT: _____

NUMBER OF DAYS SPENT: _____

WEATHER CONDITIONS

WHAT I VISITED

WHAT I BOUGHT

WHERE I SLEPT

WHERE I EAT

WHO I MET

SECTION TO MARK THE SCORE FROM 0 TO 10

0   1   2   3   4   5   6   7   8   9   10

THE MOST BEAUTIFUL MEMORY

THE CALIFORNIA TRAVELER LIFEJACKET BIBLE

Hassle-free California Trip: Avoid These 9 Common Mistakes for a Smooth California Vacation

Heading to California? Lucky you! From the towering redwoods to the majestic Sierra Nevada mountains, California is a wonderland of natural beauty. But it's also a place where the traffic can be endless, the cities a bit too crowded, and the costs of sightseeing quite steep. To help you make the most of your trip and avoid some common pitfalls, we've put together a list of mistakes many travelers make while exploring this beautiful state. By planning ahead, respecting the environment, and budgeting wisely, you can ensure your California adventure is unforgettable for all the right reasons.

1. **Underestimating Geographical Diversity:** California is a vast state with distinct regions. Often, travelers lump Northern and Southern California together, ignoring the unique attributes of each region. Ensure to research and plan your itinerary accordingly to embrace the different cultures, climates, and attractions that NorCal and SoCal individually offer.

2. **Ignoring Local Vernacular:** Every place has its local dialect and slang, and California is no exception. Brush up on some local vernacular to better understand conversations and to blend in with the locals. For instance, refrain from calling California "Cali" or San Francisco "San Fran" to avoid standing out as a tourist.

3. **Overlooking In-N-Out Burger:** In-N-Out Burger is a beloved fast-food chain among Californians. Skipping it or criticizing it might make you miss out on a quintessential Californian experience. Don't forget to explore the "secret menu" for a more authentic experience.

4. **Misjudging Weather Variability:** Despite its sunny reputation, California's weather can be quite diverse. Pack layers to prepare for chilly evenings, especially in Northern California or in mountainous regions where temperatures can drop significantly.

5. **Skipping Sunsets:** California offers breathtaking sunsets whether you're by the coast or inland. Make time in your schedule to catch a few; it's a free and deeply rewarding experience.

6. **Underpreparing for Traffic:** Traffic, especially in major cities like Los Angeles, can be extremely challenging. Allocate extra time for travel, consider using public transportation, or explore carpool options to mitigate the stress of traffic.

7. **Expecting Celebrity Sightings:** While it's home to Hollywood, spotting celebrities in California isn't a guarantee. It's better to focus on the state's many other offerings rather than hunting for stars.

8. **Neglecting Natural Wonders:** Beyond urban attractions, California is rich in natural beauty. Make sure to visit national parks like Yosemite, Joshua Tree, and the Redwood National State Park to immerse yourself in California's diverse natural scenery.

9. **Disregarding Fire Safety:** Forest fires are a serious threat in California. When camping or smoking outdoors, adhere to all fire safety regulations to protect both yourself and the beautiful landscapes around you.

10. **Failing to Budget Accordingly:** California can be expensive. Budget for accommodations, food, attractions, and small expenses like bag fees at grocery stores to avoid financial stress during your trip.

11. **Overlooking Local Wines:** California is a renowned wine-producing state with many award-winning vineyards. Skipping the local wine experience would be a missed opportunity to savor some of the world's finest wines.

By avoiding these common mistakes, you can ensure a more enjoyable and authentic California adventure, appreciating the richness and diversity the state has to offer.

Absolutely loved your California Bucket List Guide?

Help others make the most of their trip by leaving a review!

Sharing your experience doesn't just take a few minutes, but also plays a crucial role in helping travelers choose the perfect guide.

Your insights will help them plan an epic California adventure, avoiding tourist traps and hitting all the must-see spots. Your review can make all the difference to someone else's vacation!

Go to the orders section of your Amazon profile and leave your feedback if this guide was helpful for your California trip!

FREE DOWNLOAD!

Sign up for the **Telegramletter** list to receive free content and interesting updates,

and get right now a free copy of the Guide

"California Season-by-Season 2023/2024"!

Click on QRcode below to join the **Telegramletter** and

download it for free!

Recommendation

Visit the link from your smartphone or laptop for a better experience.

Made in the USA
Las Vegas, NV
18 December 2023